Psychoanalytic Horizons

Psychoanalysis is unique in being at once a theory and a therapy, a method of critical thinking and a form of clinical practice. Now in its second century, this fusion of science and humanism derived from Freud has outlived all predictions of its demise. **Psychoanalytic Horizons** evokes the idea of a convergence between realms as well as the outer limits of a vision. Books in the series test disciplinary boundaries and will appeal to scholars and therapists who are passionate not only about the theory of literature, culture, media, and philosophy but also, above all, about the real life of ideas in the world.

Series Editors
Esther Rashkin, Mari Ruti, and Peter L. Rudnytsky

Advisory Board
Salman Akhtar, Doris Brothers, Aleksandar Dimitrijevic, Lewis Kirshner, Humphrey Morris, Hilary Neroni, Dany Nobus, Lois Oppenheim, Donna Orange, Peter Redman, Laura Salisbury, Alenka Zupančič

Volumes in the Series
Mourning Freud by Madelon Sprengnether
Does the Internet Have an Unconscious?: Slavoj Žižek and Digital Culture by Clint Burnham
In the Event of Laughter: Psychoanalysis, Literature and Comedy by Alfie Bown
On Dangerous Ground: Freud's Visual Cultures of the Unconscious by Diane O'Donoghue
For Want of Ambiguity: Order and Chaos in Art, Psychoanalysis, and Neuroscience edited by Ludovica Lumer and Lois Oppenheim
Life Itself Is an Art: The Life and Work of Erich Fromm by Rainer Funk
Born After: Reckoning with the German Past by Angelika Bammer
Critical Theory Between Klein and Lacan: A Dialogue by Amy Allen and Mari Ruti
Transferences: The Aesthetics and Poetics of the Therapeutic Relationship by Maren Scheurer
At the Risk of Thinking: An Intellectual Biography of Julia Kristeva by Alice Jardine and edited by Mari Ruti
The Analyst's Desire: Ethics in Theory and Clinical Practice by Mitchell Wilson (forthcoming)

THE WRITING CURE

Emma Lieber

BLOOMSBURY ACADEMIC
NEW YORK • LONDON • OXFORD • NEW DELHI • SYDNEY

BLOOMSBURY ACADEMIC
Bloomsbury Publishing Inc
1385 Broadway, New York, NY 10018, USA
50 Bedford Square, London, WC1B 3DP, UK
29 Earlsfort Terrace, Dublin 2, Ireland

BLOOMSBURY, BLOOMSBURY ACADEMIC and the Diana logo are
trademarks of Bloomsbury Publishing Plc

First published in the United States of America 2020
This paperback edition published in 2021

For legal purposes the Acknowledgments on p. xiv constitute an extension
of this copyright page.

Series design by Daniel Benneworth-Grey
Cover image © Erica Roe

"The Last Thing I Want," © Aaron Crowell, is reprinted by permission
of the author

Bloomsbury Publishing Inc does not have any control over, or responsibility
for, any third-party websites referred to or in this book. All internet addresses
given in this book were correct at the time of going to press. The author and
publisher regret any inconvenience caused if addresses have changed or sites
have ceased to exist, but can accept no responsibility for any such changes.

Library of Congress Cataloging-in-Publication Data
Names: Lieber, Emma, author.
Title: The writing cure / Emma Lieber.
Description: New York: Bloomsbury Academic, 2020. | Series: Psychoanalytic
horizons; volume 12 | Includes bibliographical references. |
Summary: "A hybrid work of psychoanalytic autotheory that tells a story about the
end of an analysis and the end of a marriage"– Provided by publisher.
Identifiers: LCCN 2019046508 | ISBN 9781501360169 (hardback) |
ISBN 9781501360183 (ePDF) | ISBN 9781501360176 (eBook)
Subjects: LCSH: Lieber, Emma. | Psychoanalysts–Biography. |
Psychoanalysis. | Autobiography–Psychological aspects.
Classification: LCC BF109.L535 A3 2020 | DDC 150.19/5092 [B]–dc23
LC record available at https://lccn.loc.gov/2019046508

ISBN: HB: 978-1-5013-6016-9
PB: 978-1-5013-7072-4
ePDF: 978-1-5013-6018-3
eBook: 978-1-5013-6017-6

Series: Psychoanalytic Horizons

Typeset by Deanta Global Publishing Services, Chennai, India

To find out more about our authors and books visit www.bloomsbury.com
and sign up for our newsletters.

For Aaron
With All My Love to Martin and Theodore

"Love's atopia, the characteristic which causes it to escape all dissertations, would be that *ultimately* it is possible to talk about love only *according to a strict allocutive determination*; whether philosophical, gnomic, lyric, or novelistic, there is always, in the discourse upon love, a person whom one addresses, though this person may have shifted to the condition of a phantom or a creature still to come. No one wants to speak of love unless it is *for* someone."

"Yet, except for the case of the Hymn, which combines the dedication and the text itself, what follows the dedication (i.e., the work itself) has little relation to this dedication. The object I give you is no longer tautological (I give you what I give you), it is *interpretable*; it has a meaning (meanings) greatly in excess of its address; though I write your name on my work, it is for 'them' that it has been written (the others, the readers). Hence it is by a fatality of writing itself that we cannot say of a text that it is 'amorous,' but only, at best, that it has been created 'amorously,' like a cake or an embroidered slipper."

"To know that one does not write for the other, to know that these things I am going to write will never cause me to be loved by the one I love (the other), to know that writing compensates for nothing, sublimates nothing, that it is precisely *there where you are not*—this is the beginning of writing."

"(One does not give merely an object: X being in analysis, Y wants to be analyzed too: analysis as a gift of love?)"

~Roland Barthes, *A Lover's Discourse*

"That one cannot then speak about love, but that one can write about it, ought to strike you…The best thing in this curious surge that is called love is the letter."

~Jacques Lacan, *Seminar XIX*

"I have dreamt of a letter…"

~Sigmund Freud, *The Interpretation of Dreams*

CONTENTS

PREFACE

This is not the book that I intended to write.

That isn't quite true. As you will see, I wrote this book because I needed to write a book. This isn't to say that it didn't matter to me what book I ended up writing, or what its content would be. It did very much, so much so that I worked on a different book—*the wrong book*—for several years before finally putting it down. I knew that there was another book that I would have to write first, though I didn't know what it would be.

So when I say that this is not the book that I intended to write, I only mean that when I sat down to write this book, I really had no idea what would come out. I approached the writing much like I do a psychoanalytic session: I started, and I waited to see what would come next. I trusted that the force of whatever was motivating me to write such that what emerged would form something, if not whole, or entirely consistent, then at least that followed a certain logic to its logical end.

I believe that that is the case, though, as with a psychoanalytic session, it is hard for me to say exactly what happened, in the writing of this book. I mean I know of certain things that have happened, as a result of this writing—certain things that I couldn't predict, though I should have been able to. Like speaking, writing is performative; when one does something with words, one acts on oneself as much as—perhaps more than—on one's readers, or listeners. This is one of the precepts of psychoanalysis. Be that as it may, it is still astounding to me that I needed to write this book in order to make possible these things in my life that I needed to happen, and that it was writing specifically that allowed for these events. But maybe this is always how it goes, with writing.

One of the things that I believe the writing of this book has done is that it has made it possible for me to become a psychoanalyst. Many things are required, officially, in order to become a psychoanalyst: various educational degrees must be received, various numbers of hours of clinical work and supervision must be logged, various courses must be attended and passed. In New York, where I live, psychoanalysis is under the purview of the state, and I am currently well on my way to receiving a New York State License in Psychoanalysis, which will allow me to practice, so to speak, legally. Yet all of the licenses in the world cannot make you a psychoanalyst. This is not to be coy about what it means to be or become a psychoanalyst, as though it is a mystical procedure. Rather, it is to follow the ethic of Jacques Lacan, who thought that every analyst must authorize him or herself as an analyst—that a psychoanalyst is only born once someone has followed her own specific logic to its end, such that she can say, I am an analyst. The moment of that articulation, as it rests on the logical edifice that precedes it, is key.

I say that becoming a psychoanalyst is a logical procedure—rather than, say, an educational one, or a legal one—because I believe it is a form of becoming that depends on psychic dynamics that are different for each person who undertakes it, and specific to the structure of each future analyst's constitution and history. It is a rather bizarre thing to become a psychoanalyst these days; whatever it is that is motivating one to do so must be rigorously accounted for. This means—and I am following Lacan again here—that an analyst can only be born from within the cauldron of her own analysis, and that self-authorization must be intimately bound up with that process.

Thus for Lacan, as you will see later, the moment of one's self-authorization as an analyst requires that one give a testimony of one's own analysis. This testimony then serves as a kind of supplement to the analysis itself as it will have produced an analyst; yet it is only with that testimony that the analysis is retroactively configured as a process that was always pointing toward the making of an analyst. One of the revolutions of Freudian psychoanalysis was its articulation of *nachträglichkeit* as a description of psychic temporality; often (problematically) translated into English as "deferred action," Freud's *nachträglichkeit* describes at times a temporal operation whereby an event lies latent, unregistered, until a later event activates its psychic potential, and at times a more radical retroactive procedure whereby a later event seems veritably to create an earlier one, as event. Lacan's *après-coup* refers to this more radical figuration.

This then is the status of supplementation in psychoanalysis, whereby a registration ex post facto creates a meaning that, as Jacques Derrida says, "was never present, whose signified presence is always reconstituted by deferment, *nachträglich*, belatedly, *supplementarily*: for *nachträglich* also means *supplementary*." As Derrida points out, *nachträglich* further means appendix or postscript, and thus *nachträglichkeit* is an effect of writing, and specifically of writing as it is addressed to another, like in a letter. This book, which is both a testimony of my analysis and an epistolary gesture—a letter with various addressees and various postscripts—is then precisely this kind of written supplement: not so much the end of an itinerary as my analysis charted it, but the flowering of a process that only properly came to be at the moment of writing.

Like all postscripts, Derrida came late in the writing of this book, as much as I knew well that he was there all along. I have always had the problem of creating my sources, especially the ones I love, before I actually read them seriously, and so I only thought to engage Derrida on the relationship between psychoanalysis and writing after I had already basically finished *The Writing Cure*. Needless to say, from that position, he hit very hard. Derrida shows us the ways that the talking cure is an effect of a writing that is that of the psyche—since in "A Note Upon the 'Mystic Writing Pad,'" in *The Interpretation of Dreams*, and elsewhere, Freud figures the psyche and its registrations as a kind of writing—and of Freud himself. The field of psychoanalysis originated in Freud's writing; it was born out of his distinctive writing practice. There may have been other ways to transmit psychoanalysis in those early days—Lacan, for example, primarily gave spoken seminars—but presumably it is significant that Freud was a writer.

Derrida is further attentive to what he calls "the sociality of writing as drama," and to the implications of Freud's own epistolary gesture—that is, his letters to Wilhelm Fliess as the place where he developed many of the ideas that would become foundational to psychoanalysis. Freud created psychoanalysis by writing of himself: by performing a self-analysis in writing and by addressing it, in part, to another. The profound intimacy of this act created an entire discursive field. There is something boggling in this, so much so that Derrida's question about it stands alone without yielding any real answer: "How can an autobiographical writing, in the abyss of an unterminated self-analysis, give to a world-wide institution *its* birth?" This then is not so far from the question that I am asking in *The Writing Cure*: How can an autobiographical writing, in the abyss of a terminating analysis, give a person—an analyst—*her* birth?

Psychoanalysts—at least these days, and in the United States—do not tend to write memoirs, in part because of a supposed injunction within classical psychoanalysis that the analyst not engage in activities outside of the clinic that might make something of herself known to her patients. This despite the fact that psychoanalysis began in autobiographical writing, and its publication. An analyst can only act as such if she has undergone her own analysis, and engaged profoundly with her own story; it is only in the space of that engagement that psychoanalytic theory means anything at all. To the extent that writing is important for psychoanalysis, I think that psychoanalysts are actually distinctively tasked with, like Freud, instantiating themselves in the scene of their own writing, in whatever form that takes. To do so can be very exposing, which Freud knew well. It's an embarrassing thing, to become a psychoanalyst. Yet revealing something of oneself can also be done rigorously, with the aim of creating an opening. It can be done by taking on the ethic of the psychoanalytic process itself, with its deep commitment to the specificity of each individual's discourse, and with the expectation that it is precisely by way of attention to that specificity that something like theory might emerge.

In *A Lover's Discourse*, Roland Barthes writes that the intention of that book is to convey "a portrait—but not a psychological portrait; instead, a structural one which offers the reader a discursive site: the site of someone speaking within himself, *amorously*, confronting the other (the loved object), who does not speak." The distinction between a psychological portrait and a structural one is, I think, key to *The Writing Cure*, with its wager that psychoanalytic writing might be done amorously—that it might, by means of an address (I to you, whoever I and you may be), create a discursive site that makes the project a structural rather than purely personal one. Not that such a project is really any less revealing.

This kind of psychoanalytic writing may also be aided by the current textual moment, which has seen the rise of autotheory, a genre that has been gaining increasing prominence in recent years (and that is not unrelated to Barthes's textual interventions). Maggie Nelson, in an interview, claims she stole the term "autotheory" from Paul Preciado's *Testo Junkie* to apply to "autobiographical writing that exceeds the boundaries of the 'personal'"; in North America, it has been identified variously with Nelson, Preciado, Chris Kraus, Ta-Nehisi Coates, Mari Ruti, and other writers. Some people have considered this kind of confessional prose to be a quintessentially feminine—or feminist—form of writing, though it is not only practiced by women, and it has also been influenced by queer writing. This is not to say that writing that merges the personal and the critical is in any way new; the practitioners of autotheory that I have read are well aware that there is a long lineage of critics who have written personally. What may be distinctive about this "new wave" of autotheory, though, is that much of it combines autobiography with so-called high theory: that is, Lacanian theory, French poststructuralism, and deconstructive theory. In other words, the personal is being revived precisely in the context of the kind of theory from which it was banished in the 1960s and 1970s. This, for me, has been particularly important. It has offered me the only way I could have ever possibly imagined writing about high theory—that is, explicitly as myself.

In any event autotheory—or what Preciado calls "a theory of the self, a self-theory"—is an intervention into the writing of theory that maintains always the rigor of the writer's particular desire, with the expectation that the more precise the specification, the wider the opening. It marks an important moment in the breakdown of the dichotomy between theory and self-writing that has reigned in the critical humanities in the past few decades, in that it is a form of writing that testifies to the inseparability of theory and life. It also is probably no coincidence that many of these profoundly intimate texts—Nelson's *The Argonauts*, Kraus's *I Love Dick*, Barbara Browning's *The Gift*, which reads as theoretically-inflected autofiction—are written as letters.

It is possible to do one without the other: to live with no particular reference to theory; to theorize with no particular reference to life. Though I for one don't know why anyone would want to.

Psychoanalysis is also founded on the notion that theory and life are largely indistinguishable. Psychoanalytic theory develops from the observation of the ways that life is lived, including by the theorist. But more so, analysis as a practice, as it is informed by this theory, is absolutely inseparable from life. I say this not as a mere truism, since of course if you are in analysis, analysis is one of the things you are doing, in your life; or, since every analysis dialecticizes the events and enunciations within and outside the consulting room, so that what happens inside changes outside and outside responds in kind. Rather, I say this less as a theorist than as an analysand, and because, at what I am starting to see as the end phase of my analysis, the lines among practice, theory, and life are becoming entirely unclear to me. All of a sudden, I am seeing theory, on the streets; from the vantage point of the end, I am seeing theory in the course of the life I have been leading. I feel resident within me certain principles that I could previously mouth, but never precisely locate. At the same time, it is as though nearly everything is becoming my analysis. Occurrences and utterances in the world outside will seem to have an immediate effect, to achieve a sudden registration, as though anyone could intervene, as though everyone is my analyst.

The book that follows is an experiment in psychoanalytic autotheory. It is a text that registers my encounter with psychoanalytic theory from the vantage point of my own life, and at a point late in my analysis when the question of my taking on the position of analyst had emerged with especial force. Lacan's articulation of what it means to be an ethical creature—his notion that the ethical position demands that one never give way on one's desire—is of utmost importance for an analyst to heed, since how can we be attentive to the desire of our patients if we have given way on our own? Thus this book archives my reckoning with my desire around the coordinates of psychoanalysis, writing, and love: a reckoning that, to use the future anterior, will have made possible both the end of my analysis and my assumption of the ethical position of analyst. It will have been an event that points in the direction of cure: my way of writing my cure, or of writing myself toward it.

Unlike almost all of my previous writings, I did not plan out how this book would go. As you will see, its structure was born from a conversation with my husband; after that, I waited for an image with which to begin. When it came, I wrote it, and then I kept writing, on and on, until I was done. I wrote in subways, in hotels, in parks, in bed, in my analyst's waiting room. I wrote at three in the morning and ten at night. I wrote anytime and anywhere; nothing could distract me; I needed no notes, hardly any preparation. I wrote what was asking to be written and didn't look back. The first paragraph I wrote—the image that commenced the series—described a dream of me and my analyst, holding a baby. Holding our baby.

ACKNOWLEDGMENTS

I am enormously grateful to Michael Levine, who has served as a guide in both theory and life since we were seated next to each other at lunch several years ago. The rigor and excitement of his scholarship have been nearly as inspiring as the example he sets for the ways that intellectual life can infuse the everyday. Conversations with him helped move this book forward at every stage of its gestation.

My warmest thanks to the first readers of this book. Cathy Popkin read with the same depth and enthusiasm with which she approached my work in graduate school, and which have buoyed me for many years. Hunter Robinson-Efrat and Evan Malater lent the subtlety of their psychoanalytic ears to their reading; I look forward to benefiting from the grace of their listening long into the future. Rochelle Lieber read both as my aunt and as the powerful reader and thinker that she is; from both positions, she has long served as a model probably more than either of us has known. Aaron Crowell's generosity and kindness as both a reader and a person have made writing and living possible.

I am endlessly thankful for my friends, colleagues, and fellow travelers in the pleasures and hardships of psychoanalytic formation: Erica Roe, Kerry Moore, Monroe Street, Anna Fishzon, Jason Royal, Azeen Khan, Christie Offenbacher, Julie Fotheringham, and Alvaro Moreira. That I am becoming a psychoanalyst feels intimately bound up with the fact that you are doing so too. Thank you to Martin Winn and Aleksandra Wagner, whose interventions on my psychoanalytic work have affected much more than just my practice; and to Eliana dos Reis-Betancourt for her unwavering support on the hard road of psychoanalytic training.

My parents gave me reading and writing in the first place; my brother forgave me for locking him out of my room while I was thus engaged, though I still regret it anyway. My two sons have made life feel important enough to write about. Ani Kokobobo, Alison Annunziata, Heather Green, and Thomas Keenan have been some of my dearest interlocutors and companions for the last two decades; Beth Reisman and Adina Lemeshow for almost two longer. Liza Knapp encouraged me to write in new ways, even when it felt risky. Barbara Browning's *The Gift* was the book that finally allowed me to begin this writing; that I then got to work and have martinis with her was another bestowal. Patrick Scanlon's collaboration in life and work has opened up both in ways I could not have imagined. His creative energy and intellectual courage motored this book from the moment he entered it.

I lastly want to thank the editors and staff members at Bloomsbury, Haaris Naqvi and Amy Martin, who were an absolute pleasure to work with. Mari Ruti, a warrior of autotheory, believed in this book from the start. Thank you for making possible what I wasn't sure was until you did: the publication of a book born of desire.

Chapter 1

ON COMING TO WRITE, OR, TELL ME ABOUT YOUR MOTHER

I conceived this book on my birthday. My husband helped a little bit—just the slightest insemination, which seems to be what I ask of him. I told him some things I had been thinking for a long time and he said, "That could be a book." Which only means, what my husband gave, what perhaps he has always essentially given, was an articulation of form. Form impregnates matter; "Wherefore that which is to receive all forms should have no form" (Plato). But what is, what has ever been, the relation between the two? (Bruce Fink) Anyway, there is something wrong with that metaphor. I think I am writing this book in order to correct, for myself, that something wrong—in order, no longer, to have to wait for that form-giving gesture, much as I am also grateful for it.

My psychoanalyst was involved in the conception too, albeit remotely, which is how she always acts. We were on our way to a party where I knew we would see her. From this strange threesome, a book was born.

If I conceive a book on my birthday, is it mine or my mother's? Is it mine, or me? Am me mine? My logic gets twisted here, along with the grammar, subject or object, and the biology, conception or birth. The timing of the book's conception was probably intended to continue twisting that logic—just enough to finally get out of it. Maybe you can twist and twist a knot so much that it just . . . falls away.

My aunt, a linguist, once told me about verbs that become nouns (I'm sure that's not how she phrased it) by shifting the accent from the second to the first syllable. Somehow, I retained this teaching as pertaining primarily to words having to do with trash: compost, refuse, object. It has taken me a long time to see that my feeling of being excluded from the world's interesting doings is the result of my own defenses, refusals, objections. In analysis once, speaking of this, I remember saying, the way you become the abject is by shifting the blame.

*   *   *

As with everything, I did my best to make the writing of this book impossible.

My favorite story about living in Russia is about when I had to renew my student visa. I went where I was told to go by the institute I was studying at—down a back alley, up the stairs of a ramshackle building, into a hovel of an office where an extremely bearded man sat ashing his cigar on a pile of papers. I said, I'm here to renew my student visa, and he said, you can't renew your student visa until you get a migration card. What's a migration card?—I asked. It's a new document, a new regulation—foreigners need one when they're walking around, to show to the police if they're stopped—he said. How do you get a migration card?—I asked. You get one on the plane, when you're entering the country. Are you leaving and coming back any time soon?—he asked. Indeed, I was, on a brief trip to London before returning to St. Petersburg. Ok, he said—you'll get a migration card when you return, and then you can come back here with it, and I'll renew your visa. It wasn't until I was halfway down the street that I realized: I can't leave the country with an expired visa.

This, as I understand it, is the paradox of the parents' bedroom in a nutshell: you can't leave until you've entered; you can't enter until you've already left.

The same structure pertained to my image of writing a book for quite a while. When I finally decided to put aside the book about the subject of my graduate degree—literature, especially Russian—in favor of writing something more personal, something attempting to give shape to the process of an analysis as I have been experiencing it for a very long time, I thought, maybe I'll write on the idea of cure. But my plan established a neat futility, since how could I write on cure if I wasn't already cured? I'd have to wait until I had finished my analysis to begin writing. What I couldn't see was that the something "not right" in myself that I thought was motivating my analysis and preventing me from writing was simply my insistence that as yet I could "not write." It didn't occur to me that the writing was itself the righting, or something of the cure, which was what the question of writing a book always evoked for me.

Early in my analysis I dreamed of a book ostensibly written by my analyst: its cover was baroque, with a title that curved like the dome of a church. It was called *Archangels and Demons*, and it identified my analyst, after her name, as "woman psychoanalyst, and potential theologian." All of the things that it was impossible to be, she somehow was, down to the movement of potentiality, and desire. Becoming a psychoanalyst is only an achievement insofar as it opens to elsewhere.

That I identified these impossible positions as that which *she* either *was* or *had* was my neurotic deadlock. Of course, the book was mine. I had dreamed it. For crying out loud, everyone is a potential theologian. The end of analysis may well be a new way of writing oneself: an aesthetic event, it is not not-me. I made it myself but not alone; its making takes place in the space of address. The paradox of the process of analysis, which is the paradox of *nachträglichkeit*, is that with another you write yourself as the book that you will have been, but will no longer continue to be, once you have written it.

And yet, this does not mean, writing your autobiography; rather, an engagement with the unconscious puts to question the status of autobiography or self-writing (as though it wasn't already). As Shoshana Felman writes, Freud's theory of dreams—or more precisely, for her, the experience of the dream session—reveals the ways in which these unconscious productions "tell . . . us *about our own autobiography another story* than the one we knew or had believed to be our own." The dream inheres in its own telling, and its theorizing makes for "a *revolution* in the very *theory of autobiography.*" Freud's discovery of the "meaning" of dreams—wish-fulfillments—was made in the context of a dream (the dream of Irma's injection) that itself inscribed Freud's wish to discover the meaning of dreams, to theorize the unconscious, to say something about femininity, to birth psychoanalysis. The dream turns around this vortex where theory and autobiography meet, where autobiography gestures at a narration that happens elsewhere, despite us. Autobiographical accounts that imbricate stories of one's analysis, as this book in part will be, function in this matrix, perhaps just barely closer to the edge of elsewhere.

To the extent that an analysis far exceeds what is said within it, or obtains as an effect of the accumulation of sayings that outlies both the content and the register of enunciation, the book of one's analysis is hardly a rehearsal of that process. If the book lies in the direction of the cure, it can only do so as an effect of the analysis of which it is a residue, at the same time that it structures the possibility of an exit from the narrative that one tells, with its surplus of meanings. Thus the status of signification, at the end of an analysis, has started to shift—enough of the unlanguaged having been brought to language so as to change that unlanguaged field, and the pressure it exerts. One begins to see, dimly, the prospect of another relation to speech, to complaint, to responsibility, to love. And if the analyst represents the possibility of representation, then the book of an analysis must itself represent the possibility of replacing that position with something of one's own, the remainder of the process. Once the signifiers are worked and reworked and linked and unlinked and relinked and drained and voided, fallen in exhaustion, flattened of their charge, having served their purpose, enough is enough, something else happens. Somehow, from within that ongoing telling where one still needs that object—the analyst—to structure that labor, one must begin to write.

When I first started analysis, when I needed analysis so badly and so quickly that the prospect of one day ending it struck me with utter horror, I thought, well, when I terminate, I will give my analyst a book. I wondered which one: *The Brothers Karamazov*? *The Wind-Up Bird Chronicle*? *Housekeeping*? It didn't occur to me that I could be its author, or that by the time of its offering, its being for her could have, really, nothing very much, any longer, to do with her.

*   *   *

In a fit of self-reproach the other day—why haven't I done more with my life? Why haven't I written a book yet? Why isn't the book I want to write already written?—I found myself googling myself. Maybe everyone does this every once a while, as a form of self-assurance. Look! When people look you up on the internet, this is what they see! Look at everything you've done! Look at all the articles you've written! Look at how competent you seem! That's you! What a big girl you are! Google, which offers a self-reflection in letters; the internet, the mirror stage (Lacan) for literate grown-ups. It's horribly embarrassing.

What was amazing to me in this shameful act of self-research was the discovery that I had, in fact, already written a book. It's there on Amazon, and on Google Books: *God's Children* by Emma Lieber, published in 1921. It seems to be part of a series of "lost classics": old and underestimated books that have been rehabilitated and republished by a publishing house called Forgotten Books. Talk about the mirror stage in letters: your book *is* already written, it was underestimated once but now it's seen for what it really is! But heed well: it was written by someone else. Your double, your old and future self—whole, capable, finished, adult—already exists, but you're not it. And, it's forgotten.

Evidently, *God's Children* is an impassioned call for parents to talk to their children about sex, to include their kids in the scene of knowledge and desire. Evidently, it offers an implicit—or maybe explicit, I don't know, I've only read a few pages online—association between sexuality and grace (even as it also includes some extremely distasteful moments about the suppression of carnal appetite and the achievement of racial purity). I don't know if my dream book, *Archangels and Demons*, which itself presaged this present book, *The Writing Cure*, was a reference to that book, *God's Children*, which I may very well have seen years ago during an earlier fit of google-despair. It seems plausible. In which case, *The Writing Cure*—an attempt, in part, to explain to my children, whether or not they will ever read it, something about the conditions of their becoming as it was bound up in my analysis, and also, about desire as a figuration of grace—will be the fulfillment of a dream book from the beginning of my analysis, itself the residue of a forgotten book written by a me who is also a past me or perhaps a future me but in any case a not-me.

*   *   *

The end of an analysis does indeed call for testimony.

For Lacan, and the school he established in Paris in the 1960s, the procedure that accounted for this call to testimony was called "the Pass." Pass, as in, pass something along, like language. You think you're coming to the end of your analysis, and you're in a school to become an analyst, because that's what you want to be, so you call upon two other analysts-in-formation to whom to give the account of your analysis. They then pass along what they assimilate of your telling to a committee, which decides on its basis whether you are in fact an analyst. Somehow, in that process of offering your testimony to traverse the mouths of others, you usher yourself to the position of analyst which the committee then affirms.

Invectives abound against this procedure of the Pass, which is quite beautiful in theory but probably terrible in practice. Perhaps it should be taken more as a provocation to theory than to practice—except that theory and practice in psychoanalysis are absolutely intertwined. And anyway, the putting to practice of theory in schools calls for regulation, and regulation then becomes the problem. There may be no way out of this loop.

At least, the Pass testifies to the extent to which becoming an analyst is a communal project. It is done with fellow travelers. The Pass further puts into play the status of testimony, or the ways in which one's story takes on new property in the moment of its address. Felman emphasizes this necessary address in her work on testimony in law, literature, and psychoanalysis, and claims that no one can testify to your story, but you. You must address your story—to the courtroom, to the wider culture—and in so doing you must claim it, as yours alone. "There is only one specific person, one specific subject who can bear witness to what he/she has experienced, and no one else can report what this particular subject has lived and narrated."

I don't know that these two positions—only you can tell your story to the judge; only others can tell your story to the judge—are as opposed as they seem, especially to the extent that judgment isn't really, in the end, what's at stake. Rather, what is at stake is the effect of the act of testimony, and the complex place at which testimony lies in the linguistic passages between self and others. At least in theory, the structure of the Pass dances around the question of regulation only to belie it, the fact and form of address shifting entirely the status of plaintiff, witness, and judge. Probably, these positions are dialectical corollaries of each other: only I can tell my story, but I cannot tell it alone. The address itself encodes this truth; if you want to stick some others in there to mediate further—if you want to track the effects of the testimony on its way through one more round of address—so be it. But probably, the essence is the same.

I'm studying at a psychoanalytic institute that does not have the procedure of the Pass. That's fine by me. I don't think it will be up to a school to adjudicate. I suppose I am offering this book at what feels to me to be the tail end of my analysis, as a form of address to anyone who will have it. I suppose that I am writing it as a way of posing a question to no one in particular, in the hopes that the book itself will provide the means of finding an answer which only I can find but which I cannot find alone. I suppose that in the end, the book will at least have posed the question: Am I an analyst?

*   *   *

Dan Gunn's *Wool-Gathering, or How I Ended Analysis* is a book about ending a six-year analysis with a Lacanian analyst in Paris at the same time that transit strikes are overtaking the city. Gunn writes of a certain Lacanian formulation of the course of an analysis, that

> the patient starts . . . by speaking to himself; goes on to speak to the analyst but about one who is not himself; but that when he will have spoken to the analyst about himself—who will have changed in the interim by this very fact—then the analysis will be over.

Gunn describes being about a year into analysis, and falling briefly in love with an Italian woman, with whom he spends days speaking

Italian. Except, he doesn't know Italian. "Words are streaming out of my mouth which I have no recollection of ever having heard before." He manages to use the word "anzi"—a tricky conjunction as he describes it, meaning both "what is more" and "or rather"—in the context of proposing that they sleep together, and she accepts, but at that point her response doesn't matter, because he has for the first time used the word "anzi." "Here too is language, and it's speaking all by itself!"

"To end analysis . . . to end it *well*, I decided, would be to speak in such a language, or be spoken by it, in a manner both completely personal and deeply impersonal."

Gunn writes that he spends the last months of his analysis obsessing over what to write next; he has written two volumes in a triptych, and he can't seem to figure out what the third one should be about. After his analysis is over, at the very end of the book, having decamped to Bologna for a sabbatical, he is finally able to write a letter—a thank you letter, a love letter—to a woman; he faints; and he begins to write this very book, *Wool-Gathering*, the book of his analysis.

Thus the book is born of the event of the analysis's end. What would it look like to write your way to that end instead?

*   *   *

What the writer of the self knows well is that life is already made like fiction. It's not just that the writer looks back and imposes a neat or not-so-neat structure on a messy and contingent series of events. It is that she discerns the structure that already insisted from within that tangle, and makes it manifest. It hardly matters what you call the structuring party, and though psychoanalysts have proposed some names that have been variously received, what is primary in their endeavor is the conviction that this agency is the property of the person living out its effects: property in the sense that it is claimed as it is articulated, located at the moment that it is addressed, but never really there, as presence.

This does not mean that that structure is founded on or urges the recovery of any particular meaning. We may find what we consider to be meaning, lots of meaning, too much meaning, within it, but meaning-making is a secondary process for us, as creatures who get off on it. What is at the center rather is a void that is the subject, effect, and gift of language.

Consider the personal essay "I Bought a Bed" by Donald Antrim. The author's mother dies, and in the weeks and months that follow, the author tries, struggles, hopes, and fails to buy a bed. He goes from store to store, lying on beds with his girlfriend and other friends, obsessing their relative quality and price, "learning more than I ever thought I would about mattresses," fantasizing about the kind of man he would be in the bedrooms with the beds he is considering, driving salespeople and store managers and company owners mad. One says: "If you get a bed and you don't like it you can send it back. Look. You have thirty days. People send beds back all the time. That's what department stores are for." In other words, department stores are for returns.

There are various meanings to be found in these returns, some of which the author expresses, some of which he implies. He is living out something of the problem of filiation. He is researching his mother, exploring her body, figuring something out, learning more than he ever thought he would, after her death. He is surpassing her, buying a huge and luxurious bed in response to the crappy twin hospital cot on which she died. He is repeating her, practicing her craft, outfitting a mattress with sheets and ruffles and tassels and drapes the way she outfitted actors for the theater and, later, herself, for daily life—the writer of text trying his hand at textile. He is liberating himself from her ("At last, I'm free of that woman! Now I'm going to buy a great bed and do some fucking and live *my* life"): he who had essentially shared her bed, been her man, after his father left. But those were the words ("now I can live *my* life") that she herself had uttered after *her* mother's death, a year before her own. He is purchasing a roomy coffin to share with her, I'm coming Mommy, wait for me! He is resuscitating the sick bed that she occupied as a child to oblige her mother (Munchausen by proxy); that she occupied as she died and he sat watch; and that he occupied as a child as she sat watch (asthma)—obliging her by sickness, sharing in her sickness, but rebelling all the while, she is suffocating me, I can't breathe. He is killing himself as she killed him, as her mother killed her, as he killed her, with morphine and neglect and love. He is nuzzling up to her, climbing on top of her, since of course the bed that is "peculiarly soft," the one that makes you feel so relaxed it is "alarming," the one he actually keeps in his apartment for a few days, is her. A mattress so comfortable, it will be the last one you ever buy.

He is telling a story of returns, the "story of my mother and me, my mother *in* me," the story of how we hold onto mothers the way they once held us, of how we let them watch us die because they are dying, of how they make everything impossible not so much because they are difficult women, though they may be that, but because there is a structural impossibility at work: "I was never to leave her for another woman—even as this required my having . . . a succession of women. . . . I was to have a powerful cock and, at the same time, no cock at all." And he is telling this story, about his mother and the purchase of a queen bed, because it is important to tell, because it is true, because it is meaningful, but also because the other story, about the father, about the king, is, as he says, far less forthcoming.

All of this does nothing but rehearse the brilliance of the essay, and it is brilliant. But so is every person's unconscious, which is all that a psychoanalyst is there to testify to. The structure of the essay is the structure of the event—death of mother, search for bed—which was itself an effect of something profound, or rather of many, many profound things. Call them what you like: the Oedipus complex, the incest taboo, the repetition compulsion, intergenerational trauma, Eros, the death drive. The sick family, the sick woman, the sick child. The son's guilt; the search for home. Love, death, creativity, art. Find the meaning in it that interests you, the archetype that suits your purpose—it's all there. But at the center of the essay, at the center of the structure, is the gaping void of a meaningless rhyme (matricide, mattress), the ridiculous nonsense of aural resonance that creates the speaking subject and its labyrinthine structures, as well as the rather silly fact that Antrim's mother's maiden name, the last name of her father, the first person to die in the essay, was Self. Somehow, the history of a memoirist is in part determined there, in the vicissitudes of that name, though in and of itself the name, located like all selves are in a social network, words linking to other words ad infinitum, means nothing. To find the ability to love and work from the place of that nothing is, I think, the effort of psychoanalysis.

*   *   *

To tell the truth the mattress-ide joke was first told to me by my mother. It was one of her handymen who made it, as she was sliding an old mattress out of her bedroom window, for him to catch and cart away. His surprising pun as he was crushed by her old bed made us wonder if he had a crush on her. I only read the Antrim essay much later.

One of the first stories I told in analysis—when I was still telling stories in analysis—was about buying a bed. In a way, it is the reverse of Antrim's story. We bought the bed too easily, though the timing and torture of its acquirement were just as overdetermined.

It was 2008, and we were getting married in September. That summer, we visited just a couple of mattress stores on the Upper West Side before settling on the kind of offering that promises to contort itself to each sleeper's individual needs—measured, apparently, according to a number assigned by one of the store's roaming "mattress professionals." I remember wondering what it felt like to announce oneself at a cocktail party as a "mattress professional." What a vocation—to make a career calibrating sleeping surfaces such that couples don't want to kill each other. The discrepancy in numerical assignments—say you're a seventy-five, he's a forty-five—both representing, and promising a solution to, the impasse of the sexual relation. (Lacan: "There is no sexual relation.")

In any event the bed was to be perfectly matched, somehow, to each of us, the seamless mediator of our coupling, sanctioning and making possible our union while conforming precisely to our individual needs, all through the wonders of modern posturepedic technology. You really can have it all. Yet, I don't think either of us thought, in any conscious way, "Now I'm going to get married and buy a great bed and do some fucking and live *my* life!" Death, as Antrim shows us, is hardly Oedipal liberation, but surely marriage is generally even less so. And to the extent that fucking and living our lives were evoked by the announcement of our wedding, we made sure they were absolutely foreclosed too.

Because we ordered the mattress, and had it delivered to our apartment, in what turned out to be the middle of a bedbug resurgence in Manhattan, when other people were carrying around baby wipes to apply to subway seats, when seemingly everybody knew not to get a mattress delivered by mattress professionals who spent their days laboring in bedrooms across the city, carting in the new and out the old, picking up God knows what. We were blissfully ignorant of what we were doing, which meant, we knew it all too well. We got married in a small ceremony during a downpour so massive that we had trouble finding a cab and were late to the courthouse. I already had a huge bite on my forehead. Our larger wedding party was on the Amherst College campus the following weekend; on the day of the celebration, we found out that David Foster Wallace, a beloved alum who was, apparently, too married to his mother to go on living, had killed himself. On our return to New York, while we were unloading the rental car outside our building, a police van blew by us too closely and knocked off the side view mirror; the officers conferred among themselves and came back with a ticket for double parking. I was incensed but, as a lawyer, my new husband warned me: never argue with a policeman. Three days later, the stock market crashed, the subprime mortgage crisis—you can have the home of your dreams!—was revealed, and our massive bedbug infestation was confirmed.

We spent the next six months in an essentially empty apartment, all our belongings having either decamped for storage or packed into boxes in the kitchen, undergoing biweekly treatments. I wrote my dissertation staring at an empty, white wall, since we even had to take down the posters. We ran alcohol wipes over all the books—bedbugs love books. Come to think of it, I hope we applied that courtesy to all my library books before I returned them. I was writing on *Bleak House*, in which metaphors for the social network as it is compacted by urban living, as well as by the policemen who organize it, abound: infection, sludge, inheritance, money, texts, language. The city is diseased, the home is diseased, the law is diseased, the book is diseased—you can get bedbugs from the library. The treatments were undertaken by the self-proclaimed bedbug king of New York, appropriately named Cesar: business was booming, and he was in high demand, his cell phone ringing off the hook, his voice resounding in your bedroom as he simultaneously one-handed your mattress to reveal an underside littered with the fecal stains of satisfied insects and reassured another woman halfway across the city, "Don't worry honey, I'll be there in half an hour." The bedbug king who would come to the rescue, waltz into your bedroom hardly announced, before you had time to put on a bra, ask to see the bites under your clothes, and promise to solve the infestation raging in your home, burrowing its way into all your things, making you suspect every domestic object of hidden rot and bad intentions—the sickness you didn't see coming but that had been with you since the day you were born.

Thus we managed to assure everyone around us that the last thing going on in our marital bed, on the Upper West Side of Manhattan, in America, land of the free and mobile and self-made, was fucking.

Think of it according to my aunt's teaching: turn the verb into a noun, change the stress, and replace one letter. Infest.

Maybe it was better that our wedding felt like an apocalypse. Better that it was all so obvious, so clearly metaphored, so overpacked with meaning, like a novel: the violence of the state; the sickness of the Oedipal bedroom; the horror of the primal scene. Domestic bliss, a Ponzi scheme. Marriage as a kind of suicide: pure repetition, a return to the maternal embrace, she'll eat you up, you disappear into her. The bed as coveted possession and phobic object, a coffin, you'll lie on your back. The professionals, the kings and queens, who promote the fantasy of sexual alignment and enforce the necessity of heterosexual conformity. Don't worry honey. We'll make you comfortable in this bed. Within half a year, I was in analysis, telling the story of getting married and getting bedbugs, which, to add to the surplus of meaning, became itself, as narrative, an emblem of the impossibility of our pairing: "How can you explain to someone," I remember wailing, "that you think that bedbugs are psychosomatic?" I thought that a man of the law could never understand. But if this story was an emblem of the impossibility of our pairing it also, as such, presaged my desire to become an analyst, since, if an analyst is a professional, she is one who says, lie down here, on your back—lie down here, until you know that sexual alignment is absolutely impossible, because once you know that, you'll be able to live.

*   *   *

What then of accounts of analysis? (The story of becoming an analyst, as I am doing, is commensurate with the story of one's own analysis. From the other direction, the story of one's analysis is the story of becoming an analyst, even for those who do not—it is the story of acceding to a structural position that an analyst necessarily occupies but that needn't necessarily be occupied by only her. At the same time, practicing psychoanalysis does not itself guarantee that one is an analyst; something else is required. None of these are really stories, properly speaking.) What happens when someone tells something of the history of their own speech, of their own being-listened-to? What is at stake, what is conveyed? Any personal account walks the line between the particular and the general, with the understanding, not necessarily articulated, that the two have something to do with each other. Which isn't to say, you'll learn from me, or you'll see yourself in me, or you'll feel a kinship with me, or you'll embody an ideology that I propose, though those things might all happen, for better or worse. Rather, it is to say that the specificity of what is motivating me to speak is itself what is shared. Transmission *is* the transmission of desire. Psychoanalysis, by never giving up on us as we speak, day after day, year after year, can help us make something new of that gift.

In *A Dialogue on Love*, Eve Sedgwick writes that her project, as a thinker in general—but presumably it is significant that she articulates it in the context of an account of her therapy—is "to pluralize and specify." Alison Bechdel, in *Are You My Mother?*, her graphic novel about her analyses and about what psychoanalysis means to her (which is also the story of her mother and her), responds to her mother's accusation regarding the narcissism of self-writing: "Don't you think that . . . that if you write minutely and rigorously enough about your own life . . . you can, you know, transcend your particular self?" And Nancy K. Miller, in *Getting Personal: Feminist Occasions and Other Autobiographical Acts*—in which she not only theorizes "personal criticism" and explores women's autobiography but also makes her own foray into self-writing—asks: "How can you tell the difference between the merely personal and the theoretically acute? What are the grounds for establishing the difference? Who decides?"

Certainly, specification and pluralization are hardly opposed, and as Bechdel suggests, the more rigorous the specification, the wider the opening. There is nothing particularly mystical about this. But Miller's question raises another, which is, to what extent does the self-transcendent dovetail with the theoretical? This is an important question for psychoanalysis, as a field that is founded on the articulation of radical difference, but that also participates in theory-making. Where does theory fall along the continuum from specificity to generality; is it located there, or along some other rubric; either way, is it necessary? And in what way is arguing with your mother the stage for these questions?

What Bechdel's mother is accusing her of—what female memoirists have been accused of since time immemorial—is navel-gazing. An ironic indictment, since the term itself perfectly represents what is at stake: self-telling as the exploration of the site of self-transcendence, the location of sharing, the place of transmission. To speak of oneself, minutely and rigorously, is to speak of what one has received from others, since the womb. Mothers sometimes have trouble seeing their place in this, both because they are so often effaced (Freud, Marx) and also when the homage paid to them is hidden in plain sight. Bechdel is well positioned to tell this story, since like everyone, but perhaps more self-consciously than most, what she has received from her mother, along with nutrients of all sorts, is language. The biggest fight they ever had was over the pronunciation of a word. I identify heavily with this.

And yet, Bechdel knows well that within the terms of this conflict are the conditions of possibility. In giving her the play and performance of words, Bechdel's mother also gives her "the way out." What she means is that her mother shows her the way to what will become her work as an artist and writer, and how this work will make her life possible. This precisely, to Freud, is sublimation: "a way out" of neurotic conflict through a certain kind of artistic creation, or self-artistry: a self-writing, however it is effected. The inter-imbrication of life and book.

* * *

Navels, then, as points of generation and transmission: I am formed by virtue of an Other, the navel the nexus that can be apprehended but never properly plumbed. The dream navel, to Freud, is the quilting point that opens up to the abyss, where interpretation fails because, as the place of transmission, it is the place of language itself. As Lacan says, there is no way to ground language, no Other of the Other; at the place of its foundation is nothing. Felman writes that the navel of Freud's Irma dream is the nodal point at which three women in Freud's life are, in the dream, figurally layered: three women joined by a navel at the limit of language and knowledge, that limit figured in the dream precisely as the tie among women. The simultaneity of Freud's discovery, as a result of the Irma dream, of wish-fulfillment as the meaning of dreams and of the dream navel as the limit of meaning functions to undercut forms of wishful mastery—the dream's male "solutions" (semen, trimethylamine) to the problem of female desire—as they are applied to femininity and sexual difference, thus assuring that the discovery of wish-fulfillment in dreams is a wholly other kind of solution. In this sense the female resistance that provokes the dream (Irma's resistance to cure) is figured in Freud's dream paradoxically as the inexhaustibility of the unconscious, much as Irma's hysterical pain in the dream—her knot in the throat, by which she is umbilically knotted to the other women with whom she is associated—is also the knotting, nodal action of the dream navel: the dream a woman, inside of whom is another, and another.

Two years after Freud has the Irma dream, he writes to Wilhelm Fliess about the progress of his self-analysis. He had for the past three days come to a stall in his thinking, with a "feeling of being tied up on the inside," and was in despair until he realized that, twenty-eight days previously, he had experienced the exact same feeling for approximately the same amount of time. Both months, the work recommenced "punctually," on the fourth day. He writes, "From this one should draw the conclusion that the female period is not conducive to work." And yet, "The pause also had another determinant—the resistance to something surprisingly new." Freud then goes on, in the letter, to theorize, for the first time, the Oedipus complex.

What does menstruation have to do with psychic resistance? Freud says, having your period is not conducive to work—always the claim leveled at ambitious women. And yet, the pause of menstruation is also a beat before the revelation of the new; it marks the incipience of discovery, of creation. Menstruation, as a figure for both fecundity and loss—I didn't have a baby; I could have a baby—comes to stand in for the place of resistance in psychoanalysis: the extent to which, rather than representing the inability to work, it creates an interval through which work can proceed. The woman with her resistance is precisely the one who discovers the new. This all not to mention Freud's various identifications, sympathies, ambitions, and competitive feelings. How indeed can one birth psychoanalysis if one doesn't get a period?

In another letter Freud is pleased to announce that "after the frightful labor pains of the last few weeks, I gave birth to a new piece of knowledge." He had been looking for the source of sexual repression, as usual approaching himself as the object of investigation, when suddenly, on return from a holiday, his self-analysis, "of which there was at the time no sign," suddenly recommenced. A wish emerged, "That repression might be replaced by my knowledge of the essential thing lying behind it." Is the repression Freud speaks of here theoretical, or personal? To articulate the source of repression means to overcome repression enough to see its source. Psychoanalytic theory *is* Freud's autobiography.

The place of the Irma dream in Freud's theory is in part what leads Felman to underline, and to call for increased attention to, something that she calls "feminine resistance" in texts, by which she means not so much the manifest feminism of a given work but rather "a literary process of surprise" by which we come to see, unexpectedly, that the text has "effectively, unwittingly, addressed some forces, some desires, some events in our own life." Feminine resistance interpellates the reader and asks her to bear witness to her own life as the text calls to it. But this also means that autobiography (especially female) cannot be directly accessed. Rather, autobiography must take a "necessary . . . *detour through fiction.*" (As Felman quotes Woolf, "Fiction here is likely to contain more truth than fact.") Thus, we must experience *"feminine resistance as a joint effect of interaction among literature, autobiography and theory*, insofar as all three modes *resist, precisely, one another.*" And presumably when Felman says of Simone de Beauvoir that "literature, autobiography, and theory remain, . . . to the end of her career, inextricably tied together in the way in which they mutually resist and yet mutually inhabit one another," she is also talking about herself.

*   *   *

Gunn writes that dreams may indeed be puzzles, or contain wishes in the form of puzzles, but that within each puzzle is always another, on and on, with no end. He illustrates this with a metaphor taken from a Flann O'Brien novel, in which someone is given a beautiful and intricately carved chest, and the receiver of the gift can think of nothing perfect enough to put inside of it, so he carves another chest, slightly smaller, and then another, and another, each one placed carefully inside the next, the last of them "nearly as small as nothing."

*   *   *

It is always interesting to see which parent is more readily narrated in analysis. A patient will speak floridly of one parent and hardly mention another, or only speak of one by way of the other, or alternate periods speaking of one, and then of the other. Lacunae speak volumes, and though this is true of other figures as well, the parents are especially well suited to serving as screens for each other, or as points of entry into each others' stories.

These are claims that rely on a two-parent family model only on their face, since mom, or dad, or whoever, is generally also a screen for something else, even if they are the only one around.

Antrim writes about his mother because she was flamboyant and difficult and ill; because her story is a story of generational transmission whose contours are important to discern; because it is fun to talk about her. Because she is dead, because she essentially killed herself, because language is a form of mourning, because forensic analyses make good stories. But he also writes about her because his father is harder to put to language, harder to see. Bechdel writes about her father first, and *Fun Home* is a much tighter book than *Are You My Mother?* Like the story of Antrim's mother, Bechdel's father's narrative is already over— he is dead, a likely suicide—and thus there is something ready-made for narrative, not only in the sense of an ending permeating the telling but also in the obvious psychological and theoretical questions that a suicide provokes. It matters little where the narrative begins, and indeed it begins modestly enough, in a scene of father-daughter airplane, his copy of *Anna Karenina* on the floor, when Bechdel, by the look of her drawings, was around six.

It is much harder for her to begin the book about her mother. This may have something to do with what she admits was her childhood theory of reproduction, which pictured women as Russian stacking dolls: "I was an egg inside my mother when she was still an egg inside her mother, and so forth and so on." Transmission becomes difficult to trace here, beginnings as impossible to determine as endings. One can only begin at the difficulty of writing, the impossibility of beginning. And so, "This story begins when I began to tell another story." The story of the mother starts at the moment of revealing to the mother the writing of the first story, about the father—a moment that itself, in the difficulty of the announcement, repeats Bechdel's earlier coming out to her parents in a letter, shortly before she learned of her father's homosexuality, her parents' divorce, her father's death. She had figured out she was a lesbian through reading. Life and text, sexuality and writing, death and art are perfectly inter-imbricated, and they offer up a perfect conundrum, for this story of the death of a funeral home director: "Who embalms the undertaker when he dies?" Answer: his daughter, of course. To Barthes, the writer is the one who plays with his mother's body; here, the graphic novelist is the one who embalms her father's body. But the question that remains is: Does one speak of the father—in all of his impossibility, in all of his melancholy, in all of his resonance with oneself, peas in a pod, as different as can be—to explain him, to exorcise him, to honor him, but also to have a way, years later, to speak finally about the mother?

Perhaps the layering of parental narrative has to do not only with the logic of biology—with who plays what role in reproduction, with who is dead—but also with the logic of what psychoanalysts call cathexis: who is psychically latched onto and in what order, that is, the layering effect of psychosexual development as a series of identifications and attachments and translations. It would be easy to say that for both Antrim and Bechdel, in a kind of neat arrangement, the narratable parent is of the opposite sex. But this would belie the complexity of Bechdel's psychosexual link with her father—"not only were we inverts. We were inversions of one another. While I was trying to compensate for something unmanly in him ... he was attempting to express something feminine through me"—as well as of psychosexual development generally. To Freud, the girl's development is particularly tortuous; possibly for this reason, he gives it comparatively little narrative space. Boys make it seem easy. And yet who, really, is to say this is actually so?

Bechdel's father spends his life outfitting his house: a museum of things, minutely ornamented, but also a sham, garbage under glamour, real period pieces arranged around the fiction of the heterosexual nuclear family. The children were there as elements of representation: still life, family in house. But, they really lived there.

I remember my analyst saying, very early on, "The minute you start to talk about your father, you switch to talking about your mother instead." But what was I to do? There was so much to talk about—so much stuff, so many items in the traffic between us: clothes and household goods and photographs. So many things to be arranged, so many trajectories to track, so many metonyms, so many metaphors: the house, the body; retention; discharge; circulation; storage. Language, made objectal: my graduate school essays traded back and forth in an ongoing circuit of production and editing, exploring the mother's body, with the mother, inside the mother. Editing the body, tuck that in, hem that sentence, shorten that paragraph, the passage from textile to text which she rehearsed (as an editor born of garment workers) and I continued. The joys of bargain shopping. All the outsides were insides and all the words were things and so they came as such.

But what to say about a vaguely melancholic father? What things did he have to give?

Miller's king and queen stories in *Getting Personal* are called "Loehmann's: Or, Shopping with My Mother"—really a Coda to an essay about teaching women's autobiographies—and "My Father's Penis." Well, there you have it. Perhaps it's that the mother's objects are so multiple, enough to fill a department store. Two breasts, for one. And erogenous zones veritably everywhere. Something of this gives shape to, but does not put to question, the function and foundation of language. Words are not everything, but they are enough (Maggie Nelson). Whereas the father's offering exists in the gap—to Miller, "the gap in the underpants," the open fly of her father's boxers as he paraded around the house—between the symbolic and the actual, the "autobiographical penis and the theoretical phallus," which are always collapsing into each other.

This lacuna, to Miller, "brings up the question: What do I know?" What do I know about my father, what do I know about the body, what do I know about language, what do I know about sex, what do I know about theory? The mother's body begs epistemological inquiry and returns these researches tenfold. The father's may be more elusive.

* * *

Judith Butler writes:

> I do not believe that poststructuralism entails the death of auto-biographical writing, but it does draw attention to the difficulty of the "I" to express itself through the language that is available to it. For this "I" that you read is in part a consequence of a grammar that governs the availability of persons in language. I am not outside the language that structures me, but neither am I determined by the language that makes this "I" possible. This is the bind of self-expression, as I understand it. What it means is that you never receive me apart from the grammar that establishes my availability to you. If I treat that grammar as pellucid, then I fail to call attention precisely to that

sphere of language that establishes and disestablishes intelligibility, and that would be precisely to thwart my own project as I have described it to you here. I am not trying to be difficult, but only to draw attention to a difficulty without which no "I" can appear.

In *Fun Home*, Bechdel sums up something of her project by reproducing a map in the children's book *The Wind in the Willows* which, if you examine it closely, offers up images of the story's characters speeding in cars down the (fictional) streets that the map represents. "The best thing about . . . [the] map was its mystical bridging of the symbolic and the real, of the label and the thing itself"—the theoretical phallus and the autobiographical penis. This is a technique that animates Bechdel's books, especially when she draws maps, which all in one way or another refer back to the one picturing the constrictions of her father's life, his death just miles from his birth. Her drawings of her father's house then reverse the procedure: there, what is real is also artificial, material is ideation, autobiography is theory, house is map. The word at issue in the contest between Bechdel and her mother in the later book will be "ersatz."

The night after reading *The Wind in the Willows* reference in *Fun Home*, I dreamed that I was watching myself, driving a car, down a street, on a map. I was simultaneously the map-reader and the driver, which is not, in itself, unusual—people who read maps are often people who drive. What was unusual was the ontologic chiasmus: that in the space of embodiment, I was a reader, whereas in the space of text, on the map, I was a driver. This says a good deal about my chosen modes of mobility. In the dream, I was driving to my analyst's funeral. I had trouble parking.

This is all not to say that stories—of mothers and fathers and siblings; of grandparents; of friends; of first loves and rivalries and conquests; of art-making and death; of trauma—are really what psychoanalysis traffics in, though they do, sometimes, make up its meat, like in a memoir. But stories aren't actually what are at stake in analysis—not because the way we tell them is wrong (though usually it is), not because we don't have to do the work of telling them, not because you don't, at a certain point, have to stop blaming your parents for their oh-so-narratable failures, but because these narratives are insufficient as testimonies to desire and to the speech that is both its cause and effect. Psychoanalysis does not really operate on the register of narrative, with its various meanings. Instead, psychoanalysis operates on the register of performance, where language hits like a dart. It gets something done, according to the torsion of enunciation. An account of an analysis, like any personal account, will take the form of that particular analysis and that particular writer, and it will inevitably transmit something of the events at stake: the events of a life, of a psychic life, and of the long telling that rehearsed them. Possibly an analysis makes a memoirist better equipped to tell her own story, by giving her a stage for working out its structure in advance. But that's something she would be doing anyway. All an account of an analysis really does is testify to the action of desire as it motors analyses and loves and work and all the projects of living. In so doing, it also may articulate and make possible the end of analysis.

*   *   *

Who knows to what or whom "ersatz" referred, in the fight between Bechdel and her mother. One might hazard that, subliminally, it was an accusation leveled at the mother; but if it pointed to something false about the mother, it was undoubtedly doing so in reference to the father, whose manifest objects—both animate and inanimate—were shams. It's sometimes easier to blame mothers, though really it's impossible to tell who, in the parental unit, was serving whom as ersatz, as prop, or where that mutual servitude stopped and started.

But "ersatz" was also surely posing a question about the child's relationship to the parents: that is, of who is substitutable, of who gets replicated and in what way. The fight happened shortly before Bechdel was to leave for college, where she would find new objects of her own.

Andrew Parker (a family friend; as Sedgwick, who was Parker's great friend, says in her narrative of her therapy, "Hi Andy!") writes about "mother trouble," and about the ways in which the mother troubles the sites of distinction between literal and figural, singular and general, life and work: this troubling bearing in some way on "her" place, or apparent lack of place, in theory, and philosophy. Some people think there are tons of mothers, tons in mothers (Derrida: "Supplements of mothers . . . an irreducible plurality"), some people, only one. (Freud: "No one possesses more than one mother.") Some people never write about mothers, some people's never-writing-about-mothers seems suspicious. Some people write only of them. Some people think writing itself is accomplished in relation to the mother's body, a playing with the mother's body, the limit of knowledge (Barthes). Some people think the mother blots out the possibility of sense-making, the link between sign and referent, that she or her body "gnaws away at the all-mightiness of the Symbolic"; as well, that she herself must be blotted out for us to live, "matricide . . . our vital necessity" (Julia Kristeva). Some people think that women (a group that does not comprise all mothers) are inscribed in the symbolic order without exception, which also means, that women achieve a certain place in it without limit (Lacan). Some people say that the mother is at once "the one safe haven of interpretation" and "the vanishing point of all identities, where no form of knowing could ever reach" (Jacqueline Rose). Some say the mother—as sign for the body—cannot be thought. Some people say the mother cannot anchor meaning, as "the last term of a regression" (Parker), at the same time that other regressions will often bring us back to her. The question of personal criticism, writing *as a*—Can one write as a mother, especially about anything other than maternity? Some people say books are *definitely not* babies (Simone de Beauvoir). Some people say creativity is coded feminine; some say it's coded masculine; some say that's the wrong vocabulary. Some people say it's impossible to write while the baby naps. Somehow, these are all the same thing. I don't really care which side I'm on. (Right now, my kids are watching "Dinosaur Train.")

It was always confusing to me why the verb "to father" would indicate a one-time event, as though it is a singular achievement. I was caught up in its temporal obscurities: What constitutes the moment of fathering? Conception? What if the baby dies in utero? Birth? In which case, does not the one who gives birth father the child? But no, that's not right. Fathering seems to refer to some moment that can only be assigned in retrospect, after a time lag, as *après-coup*; once the child is there—however the child got there, through whatever labors—then the fathering can be located, back at the moment of insemination, in someone else. Why would I assume it was more triumphant than precarious?

Whereas, mothering seems to have no beginning, and no necessary end. It exists best in that gerundial form, infinite imperfective aspect (imperfect, like Winnicott's good enough mother) encoded in the noun As it does not refer to its own inception, it does not inscribe a necessary triangulation No one else is needed, besides the one being mothered. Birth exists somewhere in between being fathered and being mothered.

Felman writes about Freud's dream of Irma's injection as a way of interrogating the split vision of male and female reading and writing, the he said/she said of Freud writing about women and women writing about Freud—that is, as a way of articulating the ways they search for and miss each other. And also, in order to talk about Freud's desire to read women better, and to move away from injected male solutions to the problem of women's desire that the dream both suggests his practice traffics in and condemns. Thus the dream, according to Felman, avows the wish to give birth to psychoanalysis otherwise, without such synthetic solutions. Female desire is the founding enigma of psychoanalysis, and as a man, Freud cannot quite read it, competing in pregnancy as he is at the time of the dream with his wife. But at least, he wants to read women better. Perhaps, that desire is enough.

"The analytical fecundity" of the Irma dream, writes Felman, "proceeds . . . from the doctor's destitution from his mastery . . . from the *destitution*, in effect, *of mastery as such*."

"The subject of the dream is saying: I myself am a patient, a hysteric; I myself am creative only insofar as I can find a locus of fecundity in my own suffering."

"The dream is saying that for Freud to give birth to psychoanalysis, the patient . . . has first to give birth to herself: to her own therapy, to her own truth."

*   *   *

My sexual theory as a child was that babies were made in hospitals, with the help of nurses and doctors—a medical intervention. These things can't just *happen*, can they? As though their emergence in a hospital (my brother was born when I was four) retroactively situates the site of their inception. I also thought all knowledge came from taking classes. Hospitals and schools—where else can anything be conceived? I used to follow around the handymen in our home, asking them how they learned to hammer and solder, whether they had gone to school for it, desperate to know the secret of such mastery. Then, the horror: the penis gets *hard*? How on earth does that happen? I figured, they (handymen, doctors) must put it in the freezer. I'm not sure whether I thought it was detachable, for that purpose. Can I take the class too?

The moment of coming-to-know was staged over the word, not the deed—in first grade, asking my parents what "fuck" meant. My father took it that I was asking where babies come from, which he then explained—but my secret, which I have never told him, was that I already knew (a friend's parents had given her a book). The simultaneity of knowing and not-knowing—knowing the secret before the signifier for it—was shocking, though of course I "knew" nothing beyond the words for things, and also, I must have known, somewhere, that word too, otherwise how know to ask about it, how know the inevitable quickening of that asking? I suppose I was spurring my parents into that quintessential parent-child scene, giving them an opportunity to teach me what I already knew, which was also, to teach me about me, in order to keep them in the loop, keep them relevant. I suppose I could only do so via our shared appreciation for the meanings of words, and via the guise that I was only interested in signifiers. I have wondered whether all of my subsequent researches have taken on a similar structure.

I have a dear friend whose first word was "fuck." She was watching as her mother dropped something, and that's what came out. No one had to explain to her what it meant.

Parker is interested in the moments that J. B. Pontalis wonders whether mothers can be exchanged, or changed. To Pontalis, the mother is not interchangeable, and that's why we so often try to change her: by cheering her up or fixing her or talking to her or listening to her. (Some people say this is why one becomes a therapist.) But, no one can change their mother, perhaps precisely because she is not interchangeable: "There is no *ersatz* for the mother; she is irreplaceable, she is unchangeable." And yet Parker points out that Pontalis can't quite make up his mind whether the mother has singular being—whether she truly resists imitation, "if anything can" (Parker). Even being "the only one" (as Pontalis calls the mother at another point) certainly doesn't mean that she can't be imitated—maybe it ensures it. Mother can resist all "she" wants. And, if she is truly unchangeable, she does.

*   *   *

The question of ersatz is thus a question of love and so, in the context of psychoanalysis, a question of transference. As Freud says of psychoanalytic cure as an effect of work within transference, "essentially, one might say, the cure is effected through love." Psychoanalysis intervenes on our ways of loving by concentrating the question of love in the analyst and the intensity of his listening. Thus, psychoanalysis answers illness in kind, since "we are bound to fall ill if . . . we are unable to love." "In the last resort," says Freud, "we must begin to love."

Lacan writes that to Freud, there is no real difference between transference and what we call love. "On the plane of the psychic," transference in the psychoanalytic setting and love in the world outside are the same thing. It is not only that transference revives old loves and puts them on stage in the context of the treatment but that in fact "transference—is love."

Thus transference love is not ersatz, or is ersatz only to the extent that all love is ersatz in its relation to the conditions or fact of

representation. At a certain point Freud does say that the love of the
analysand for the analyst, as a repetition or copy of earlier (sometimes
infantile) love relationships, must be treated "as something unreal."
Yet he then questions almost immediately whether this is in fact the
case. Whatever is at play in transference with respect to the act of
replication is always what happens in states of love, which all in one
way or another "reproduce infantile prototypes." It is at this juncture
that Freud reaches for the kind of technical and aesthetic metaphor
that serves him so well. Our ways of conducting ourselves within
eros—the contexts, aims, satisfactions, and scenes of our erotic lives—
form a "stereotype plate (or several such), which is constantly . . .
reprinted afresh . . . in the course of" our lives. This stereotype plate is
attached to an originary object—a prototype—to which, in the context
of a treatment, the "cathexis will have recourse," introducing the
analyst into a psychical "series" that is already operative: father-imago,
mother-imago, what-have-you.

Yet what seems to be important here is not only that all of our
attachments have infantile precursors, or that we're always replicating
relations that were set down in early life—that the relation of the
analysand to the analyst is replication the same way all mature ways of
loving and relating to objects are replications—but, more so, that that
original relation or object is itself a "stereotype plate," a "prototype,"
an "imago." There is nothing beyond representation here; the original
is original only insofar as it produces copies. It is not so much that
transference love is a map or grid created and proliferated from the
singular reality of infantile relating, but that infantile life is constituted
as such by being the grounds of the reprints that will follow.

(Love is printed matter.)

Thus, when Freud does a full 180 on himself and says that in fact
transference love is "second to none," he means, transference love is
efficacious, it achieves perhaps even more than other loves one of the
aims of love, which is to change our calcified ways of loving through
a radical encounter. But I also think we can hear in this formulation
the notion that transference love is belated, and that what stands at the
front of the series that precedes it is precisely nothing, the original a
vacancy that can only come to be in deferral. And that it is an encounter
with this nothing, as it reveals the binding of representation and love,
that transference love in particular offers, and that makes it work.

This all then can be thought in the context of what Lacan formulates
as object *a*, the object that causes desire. To Lacan, desire does not so
much seek an object out there, but is rather caused by an object or

objects whose loss is foundational to subjectivity. If we think the object at stake is something to be got rather than something irremediably lost, then we are making a mistake about desire (which we generally do). He further figures these lost objects as pertaining to the body at the places where exchange, gift, and reception become apposite (breast, feces, gaze, voice), and as evoking the phallus precisely in evoking castration, or the lack in being that marks the life of the subject.

"The objet *a* is something from which the subject, in order to constitute itself, has separated itself off as organ. This serves as a symbol of the lack, that is to say, of the phallus, not as such, but in so far as it is lacking."

This object is both constitutively lost and also constitutes the remainder of the unlanguaged: it has not been colonized or recuperated by symbolization. It propels us to seek substitutes for something that was never there and whose actual emergence would constitute the collapse of the subject and its world. (In psychosis, says Lacan, the object has not been lost.) Winnicott's transitional object, which the child must abuse, sully, and lose in order to enter the social, bears domestic relation to these ideas.

In an analysis with a neurotic, the analyst takes on the position of object *a*. Like it, she becomes an objectal figuration of absence and loss, and also of nothingness, of what happens at the body's various rims where things just fall away; like it, she becomes irreplaceable for this reason, for never having in any sense been had. The analysand's transference love as it locates object *a* in the analyst is part of what makes analysis work, but so is the analyst's love as it entails taking on this position of the object which "sets us ablaze" (Fink) and which in so doing makes possible new desirous acts. This love is further founded on the expectation that at some point, that irreplaceable thing will finally be dropped in exchange for still more irreplaceable things.

Thus a Lacanian analyst never really—or very rarely—"interprets the transference" because, certainly, you don't want to cut off the branch that you're perched on; but more than that, because asserting something like "you're treating me like your mother but I am *not* her!" misses precisely the point.

*   *   *

Freud is worried about analysts responding to their patients' demands in the realm of love, particularly when an especially compelling woman "sues for" it (likely the most dangerous possibility for him). One cannot bow to erotic demands as an analyst because indulging in a tryst with a patient, say, would be to abandon the position of love that is required of the analyst. In any case who's to say what sex really has to do with any of this. Presumably, if an analyst is able to do something by way of love outside of the consulting room, he'll be less enticed to make this mistake in the face of his patient's suit.

To Lacan, a demand is always a demand for love. This certainly does not mean that satisfying a demand with its apparent object does much by way of satisfactory proof of love, which will always be demanded anew. Desire then enters into this space. "Desire is neither the appetite for satisfaction nor the demand for love, but the difference that results from the subtraction of the first from the second, the very phenomenon of their splitting." The analyst, amid the proliferation of demands, must take her place in this gap, in desire as this kind of residue.

*   *   *

Miller discusses the "story of 'coming to write'" that begins so many of the women's autobiographies that she has worked on, and the relation of this story to maternity. In many of the French writers she once studied, the two were absolutely opposed. "Coming to writing [was] at the same time . . . the bracketing of the authors' own maternal function." This may only mean that the position of writer-as-daughter was embraced instead, such as in De Beauvoir's *Memoirs of a Dutiful Daughter*. The title is ironic, at least in part, and indeed one wonders if such a thing—a memoir of a dutiful daughter—is possible. What is scarier than a daughter who writes? Bechdel writes that when they speak on the phone, her mother doesn't want to hear anything about her life. Is this because she is a lesbian, or because she is a writer? There is no escaping the embarrassment of being researched, when you have children.

But what of the "bracketing of the maternal function" (and one of the premises of Bechdel's life is that she will not have children) when the book is explicitly bound up with a rather tangled bio-logic? "It had been five months since this book was due," Bechdel writes of starting to write, "and six since my last period." Menopause, or pregnancy? Moreover, how is it that one can only write of the mother once conceiving a child is biologically out of the question? Perhaps the book refigures entirely the question of fertility. As Bechdel says to her therapist, "I can't write this book until I get her out of my head. But the only way to get her out of my head is by writing the book! It's a paradox." After a particularly heady session with her therapist, one of the characters in Bechdel's comic strip gets pregnant.

*   *   *

At some point toward the middle of my analysis, it became clear that I wanted my analyst to give me a baby. Specifically, a daughter. It came to me in an image one night, right as I was on the cusp of sleep: a vision, as if a photograph, of the two of us, standing in front of a house, holding a baby for the camera, grinning. We were standing close together, though not exactly touching—rather, our contiguity was mediated by the infant we were both gripping. I don't remember what the baby looked like, whether she was wearing anything in particular or even pictured in any specific way. What I mostly remember are our grins: grins which said, we know this is absolutely ridiculous—us together, analyst and patient, holding a baby it would be impossible for us to produce— but really, we are very happy. We are a family that makes manifest the absurdities of being a family. Having a baby, otherwise. Would that analysis could give me that ability. The image was accompanied by a verbal caption: "We would have a girl." In the session in which I described the scene, my analyst refigured it as: "We would know what to do with a girl."

*   *   *

Eve Sedgwick defines the family, queered, as "people who come or stay together because they love each other—can give each other pleasure— have real needs from each other. Not structured around blood and law. Completely different principle of affiliation."

*   *   *

Felman says that the chapter in *What Does a Woman Want?* about Freud's relation to the Irma dream was written in order to articulate something to her male analyst about herself as a woman that she felt he couldn't hear. It's hard to say what this something was, besides that it inheres in the subtlety of her readings of sexual difference and of reading as an effect of sexual difference. She writes of how Freud reads women and how women read Freud; of how Freud reads as a woman or at least wishes to read as a woman; of how women read Freud as men and perhaps misread Freud as a man—and yet he is a man, and yet they are women. She writes of the impossibility of that impasse, and yet from somewhere within it, you can write something to your male analyst.

* * *

Sedgwick begins her book about her therapy with the premise that "somehow, it is as a patient that I want to emerge." She writes that her account of her therapy will "*show [her] to be loved.*"

I started off having a hard time with *A Dialogue on Love*. The encounter between the academic and the analyst that it limns touched a nerve in me that I'm pretty ashamed of. Sedgwick wonders whether her therapist is stupid. She doesn't go to a great intellectual for analysis. She doesn't go to someone who understands deconstruction. She goes to someone whose first discernible characteristic is his "gift for guyish banalization."

I would never be mistaken for someone who engages in guyish banalization. But that's no good for an analyst: the horror of being taken as dumb. This is certainly not to glorify banalities. Rather, it is to say that the ability to be stupid is an important thing. Lacan says that being the dupe is inherent to listening well. Whatever that may mean, to allow yourself to be an object at another person's disposal, put to use in the economy of their rage and desire, is, I think, one of the phantasmatic contours of stupidity, or at least what is perhaps most feared in the fear of being stupid. Presumably, it's something Sedgwick was herself looking for, or for more of. "Fatuity"—a word in her scholarly vocabulary—couldn't not have been significant to her, as a connoisseur of fat.

And anyway, Sedgwick makes explicit what is at stake in the terror of the other person's stupidity: "I need you *to change me*. . . . Don't go being all stupid. You can't just let me drop." What she wants changed is, in part, something of the "S&M" fantasy life—beating fantasies, rape fantasies, what-have-you—that is so elaborated for her but that also raises a question about the stakes of her desire, and specifically I think about the anality inherent (and no one has theorized her own anality like Sedgwick) in both the demand to be changed and the fear of dropping. Somehow, that fantasy structure then must pose a question about being taken as an object, about being stupid.

The question that binds Sedgwick's narrative at the beginning—"*Is* Shannon stupid?"—represents her destruction of him, which he survives (Winnicott). It speaks to his skill in being used and to hers in using, the interplay of which shows her to be loved.

Segwick's horror of Shannon's stupidity may be akin to Felman's feeling of having been missed, by her analyst, as a woman, though for Sedgwick the stakes feel rather different. In any case, both were compelled to write by something of a missed encounter with a male interlocutor.

Felman on female autobiography: "Whom do we *write for?* Whom do we *wish* to be *read by?* Whom are we *afraid* to be read by? Whom do we *trust* to know how to read our writing? Whom do we need in order to *help us grasp the truth* that lies in wait (for us, for others) in our story but that alone we do not have the strength to grasp? Who can help us, or *enable us,* to *survive our story?* Who is our *internal witness?* Who is our *external witness?* Who is our *voluntary* witness? Who is our *inadvertent* witness?"

It is the impossibility of knowing "*the real addressee* of the text of our desire and of the writing of our life . . . that is, precisely, what the story of the Other is telling us each time anew and what female autobiography . . . is striving, at its most profound, to narrate."

*   *   *

At the very end of "A Poem Is Being Written," Sedgwick says that she wrote the essay in the hopes that "readers or hearers would be variously—in anger, identification, pleasure, envy, 'permission,' exclusion—stimulated to write accounts 'like' [it] . . . (whatever that means)." Perhaps she meant, that she wrote in the hopes that others would be inspired by her to write something that specifies and pluralizes, or that bridges the personal and the theoretical, the erotic and the academic. In any event, she wanted to be used.

*   *   *

How *do* you know what's inside? Do you have to know in advance? Boy, girl, short story, novel, scholarship, memoir? I found an old document on my desktop recently with ideas for short stories that I never wrote.

*Woman whose baby dies so the social fabric unravels

*Boy with a stutter whose only reliable word is "block"

   "It came out in one big blocky burst."

   "A feeling that was very much not like a block."

*Gypsies

*Collector: person who makes lists of all her friends, desires

*Woman who has a different body for every mood

*Story about a woman who has cords connecting to other people coming out of her body. Cord to mother, out of the navel, is strongest. Describe each cord (umbilical cord is thick and has sinews and veins;

cord to father has scraggly hairs; cord to sister comes out of the ankle and is surprisingly hard, like a thin bone; cord to husband is labile, sometimes smooth, sometimes brittle, needs a lot of moisturizer). For a while she walks around and feels ok, only some positions are uncomfortable, such as riding the bus when she has a lot of grocery bags. But then it starts getting more and more cumbersome. One day she climbs into a spaceship—hard to get the suit on—launching—tension, pulling at the skin, stretching in every direction—until, one by one (in what order?), they break.

One of the few short stories I ever followed through on is below. From the looks of it, like the abovementioned list, I must have written it either shortly before, or shortly after, starting analysis.

Place Settings

Emma Lieber

It was a crowded household. There were Sarah and Michael, of course, lanky both, recently married with two bright-eyed young children: Edward, 3, and Annabelle, 9 months. There was Sarah's mother, a former dental hygienist who believed in the importance of flossing in early life and who slept in the attic with the trunks of winter clothes. There was Michael's father, an ex-military man who was shaped like a pickle jar; he lived in the basement with the extra fridge. Michael's older sister, thick as a house and unhappy in love, would stay on the couch on occasional weekends and throughout the month of August.

Also in residence was Sarah's dearest friend, Elizabeth, who had grown up by her side. Pretty and demure, Elizabeth had a gentle voice, wore plain-colored dresses, and liked to sit to the right of whomever she was conversing with. And Arthur, Michael's college roommate, who had taught him to identify whiskey by smell and to protest poor service in restaurants. On very rare occasions, Michael's old girlfriend from those days would stay the night, but she would always be gone before breakfast; every once in a while Sarah would find a pair of her stockings in the communal laundry, would fold it cheerfully, and would place it on top of the basket of Michael's clothes. Then she would go strip the bed in the guest house.

She didn't mind having the bedroom to herself on those nights. She got a lot of reading done.

Recent additions included Sarah's therapist, an older gentleman with graying hair and thin lips; his wife, who was as frail as a sickly child and hardly spoke; her English master's thesis adviser, who had a Keats poem for every occasion and wore the same rust-colored sweater every day; and Michael's co-worker, Kenneth, who was never seen around the house without his briefcase. And just last week, Michael's Junior High baseball coach called from Seattle to say he would be stopping through for a while.

Dinners were noisy. At the long banquet table in the dining room everyone would take their usual places: Michael at the head with Edward on his knee; Sarah at the foot grasping Annabelle. Sarah's mother sat in the corner seat to Sarah's right, and Michael's father to his. To Sarah's left, and across from Sarah's mom, would sit Elizabeth, followed by the therapist's wife, followed by the therapist; to Michael's left was Arthur and to his left Kenneth, in between whom would squeeze Michael's sister when necessary; the English professor sat at a small side table. An empty chair was left between the therapist and Michael's dad, for when Coach arrived. Every once in a while Kenneth and Arthur would switch places.

Sarah's mother would prepare soft vegetables and tough meats and serve them with loud clanks onto carefully arranged place settings. While she bustled Michael's father would remain tensely perched, critical and fat with expectation. During the meal Arthur and Kenneth would discuss politics; Michael's father would bark at Michael's sister when she was there and Sarah's mother when she was not. Elizabeth would sit in preening attention to Sarah's every gesture and chilly ignorance of the therapist's wife to her left, who stared at her food and did not eat. The English professor would make witticisms that no one heard; the therapist would rock on his chair's back legs and gaze at the corner where the ceiling always met the wall. And every evening Michael would bounce the giggling Edward and Annabelle would clutch at her mother's forefinger.

But at night, after the plates were cleared and the cooking odors dispersed, everyone would retreat to their separate bedrooms, gently shut their doors, and nestle wearily between sweet-smelling sheets. And then they would each dream dreams that were entirely their own.

*   *   *

For some reason I seem to think that being in analysis has something to do with plagiarism. At least, it has been so for me.

There was a period of time in which everything I wrote bore something plagiarized from my analyst. Something very small—a phrase, a word, a conceit—that she had used in a session, or that I had discovered in my research of her writings. The slightest insemination, the sine qua non of writing.

In sixth grade I got caught plagiarizing. We had to write a poem for our creative writing lesson and I didn't have any ideas, so I wrote down verbatim the lyrics of a Mary Chapin Carpenter song that my mother used to listen to in the car, about a cat that has her babies on a man's shirt. It's a very pretty song and I realized as I wrote it that I knew all the lyrics by heart. My teacher was a very tall and charismatic mustachioed man in his late twenties, one of only two male teachers at the school. Everyone was in love with him but even then I found cults of personality a little creepy.

He caught me. How on earth did he know that song?

At the same time, why did I think I had no ideas for a poem? Earlier that month, under the same imperative to produce poetry, I had written a lyric about a father in a vegetarian household who beats his children, which I found to be a very neat irony. Mr. Gifford had called me out into the hallway to ask if this was a bit of nonfiction, to which I uttered a shocked dissent, stunned and a little wobbly by the scene I had created. I don't know about you but when my unconscious scenarios return to me from outside, I get very dizzy.

Plagiarism can be a method of use, a way of accounting for the distance we suffer from our objects. As in Freud's grandson's *fort-da* game (baby throwing the toy out of the crib and then retrieving it while Mommy is gone), cribbing has something to do with loss, and mourning. I remember that the penance for my misdeed was to get up in front of the class and recite the definition of plagiarism—a little embarrassing, though I actually now find it sweet, since Mr. Gifford didn't tell anyone of my offense. And, in any case, I essentially stood up and recited, verbatim, the definition I had looked up in the dictionary. As though you can really regulate the transmission of words, or fairly impose the imperative of originality. Plagiarism has, for me, been an attempt to negotiate Oedipus: a way of making myself learn that no one owns the property rights to words and that all words like all people come from someone else—that there is no original as such.

But it has also been symptomatic. Presumably you wouldn't have to steal words if you really thought that they circulated freely.

If these are my early mother and father verses (mother versus father), it is the mother (or her surrogate) who is stolen from, as a response to something dangerous in composing the father. But what was the danger in writing about such a demurring father, such that his fictionalization had to be so apparently complete, his threat made so obvious? What was it that I had betrayed; what was I asking from my reader? Plagiarizing from the woman seems to be both a restitution for that betrayal and a protection against further abuses.

In the end, what is at stake in Bechdel's memoirs is not only the Russian stacking doll of embryos inside mothers but the infinite regress of texts. These things are inter-imbricated: *To The Lighthouse* is a touchstone not only for its consideration of symbolic and actual, specific and general but also for its history as the text by which Woolf exorcised her mother. If mothers cannot serve as "the last term in a regression," the same is most certainly true of texts. Signifiers will always travel, unpredictably; the homage we pay to other speakers when we mouth their words cannot be measured. Citation, which both marks and effaces the history of that transmission, always betrays the desire that leads someone to quote someone else. I use "betray" in its two meanings, as in, does violence to, but also, reveals something nonetheless.

In graduate school we were taught never to quote a text via another text. In other words, you should never provide a quote from Hegel that you read not in Hegel, but in Kristeva; you should never reproduce a sentence of Kristeva that you read in Butler. Always go back to the source; show that you've read the original. Don't leave such a gaping flaw in your manuscript. Why? Because it's not classy? Because it makes you look like a child? Because only the precursor can speak? Because mere quotation is ersatz? What if what interests me is seeing what, in a text, turns on another writer, such that she would want to repeat those words? What if after that, I would prefer to move on?

Bechdel often "quotes" by drawing the page from the book she is referring to, and depicting the sentence or phrase at issue as highlighted. I find this very charming, because it reveals what is truly at stake in quotation. It brings the reading body into the picture, the traces of its research, the marks of its desire. In *Are You My Mother?* there is a graphic of Bechdel, in bed, with a reading flashlight attached to her head, digging into Adam Phillips's *On Kissing, Tickling, and Being Bored*: it's a profile picture, and we see the cover. She is describing a period in which she was heatedly reading books about psychoanalysis. As I looked at it, I remembered being similarly captivated by that book in high school (in fact I left it half-accidentally one night at the house of a boy I had a crush on, as a form of seduction). I wondered what it would feel like to be Adam Phillips seeing this homage to him. I wondered if he would put a print of it up on his wall—not to return the tribute, but to further promote its action.

Nelson quotes, not by literally drawing the reading body into the picture, but by divorcing the words from their speaker: in *The Argonauts*, attribution happens elsewhere, in the margins. She got the technique from Barthes, who writes that the references in *A Lover's Discourse* are

> not authoritative but amical: I am not invoking guarantees, merely recalling, by a kind of salute given in passing, what has seduced, convinced, or what has momentarily given the delight of understanding (of being understood?). Therefore, these reminders of reading, of listening, have been left in the frequently uncertain, incompleted state suitable to a discourse whose occasion is indeed the memory of the sites (books, encounters) where such and such a thing has been read, spoken, heard.

Thus what is highlighted is the metabolization of another's language, the extent to which words leave their speakers to fall into the gap between the margin and the text and are taken up in specific meetings, sites of encounter. As Nelson says, the words themselves are enough. To memorialize their origin is to pay homage to what they have done to you. The reader is understood by the text as much as she understands it. I aspire to this form of quotation.

Nelson gives us Barthes—actually, she gives Barthes to Harry, her book's addressee (along with her son Izzy), and then reports the gift to us:

> A day or two after my love pronouncement, now feral with vulnerability, I sent you the passage from *Roland Barthes by Roland Barthes* in which Barthes describes how the subject who utters the phrase "I love you" is like "the Argonaut renewing his ship during its voyage without changing its name." Just as the *Argo*'s parts may be replaced over time but the boat is still called the *Argo*, whenever the lover utters the phrase "I love you," its meaning must be renewed by each use, as "the very task of love and of language is to give to one and the same phrase inflections which will be forever new."

At the same time, "I love you" is also like Nelson's family, and its bodies: replace the parts on one, alter the hormone levels in another, change one's shape, put one in another, sever one from another, add, remove, grow, shift.

These shifts can themselves be marked by name changes, as was true of Harry (who was born Wendy and grew up Becky). But this is renaming more along the lines of the man Nelson refers to later in her book, who weds his wife under an assumed name, in order to escape his rich family. Having given them and the state "the slip," the two remain married for fifty-seven years: "Fifty-seven years of baffling the paradigm, with ardor." Long, monogamous, heterosexual marriage made subversive, by a name change.

And anyway, who knows what's going on underneath a conventional image. Nelson describes a photograph of their family at Christmas (herself while pregnant, butch-on-T Harry, and Harry's son by another nonheterosexual relationship) as, to the eye, a veritable heteronormative tableau. Nelson: "No one set of practices or relations has the monopoly on the so-called radical, or the so-called normative." Nelson on Sedgwick: "She wanted the term ['queer'] to be a perpetual excitement, a kind of placeholder—a nominative, like *Argo*, willing to designate molten or shifting parts, a means of asserting while also giving the slip. This is what reclaimed terms do—they retain, they insist on retaining, a sense of the fugitive." Nelson quoting Sedgwick: "Queer is a continuing moment, movement, motive—recurrent, eddying, *troublant*." What does it matter how you achieve this ability to move? Doing so is only the flight of the outlaw, on the lam from the family and the state, if we can't see that these tributaries are inherent in language itself. The family is only a problem when it makes that mistake, which it generally does; the state, most likely, is founded on it.

Nelson calls the people whose words she has found to be enough, "the many-gendered mothers of my heart." I have them too, and now she is one of them. Sedgwick was a many-gendered mother for Nelson and is one for me as well but, in my chronic belatedness (not fashionable lateness but late-bloomerness), Sedgwick only became my mother after she had already died. It keeps going and going, the circuit of appropriation and production and reception and rejection and gift that we play around the mother's body.

These writers have led me to each other, texts compelling you onward to other texts, like looking up words in a dictionary, the infinite regress of signification. I have taken something from all of them, in both content and form. Mostly I have been grateful for the lessons they offer in hybridity, and in the wager of self-writing, and I have imbibed from them the claim that you can reach for something that transcends the self by writing, minutely and rigorously, about yourself. As well, the insistence that one way of writing about yourself is to write the history and passions of your reading and writing, to make manifest the erotics of the academic with the understanding that to tell one's own story is also to take a detour through the stories of others. These writers have enabled me to write. Now, for the most part, I will leave them behind.

*   *   *

In a course at my psychoanalytic institute, I was recently assigned an article by an analyst named Phyllis Greenacre that ended with an encomium to the "high degree of restraint and sacrifice" that is required by psychoanalysts. Being an analyst "demands, among other things the sacrifice . . . of conspicuous public participation even in very worthy social and political 'causes' to which he may lend his name or his activities." In his quest to be the ultimate blank slate for his patients, the analyst presumably must also sacrifice writing generally, even about very worthy causes and especially about himself. The article was written in the 1950s but one does still hear such arguments.

I'm not terribly interested in getting in a fight with anyone about the sturdiness of the transference—about the ways it swallows every bit of material it can find no matter the source—or about what Freud did with his patients; or about how analysts simply have to find ways out of their own inhibitions, not to mention their masochism, both of which are served by self-restrictions of all sorts; or about how it's impossible to hide from Google nowadays, no matter how little you do. Or about how an ethical analyst is only constituted as such by virtue of never giving way on her desire, desire being not a desire for something but a structural effect of subjectivity as it is founded on loss—that is, something that keeps you moving in the field of causes you find worthy. Or about how an ethical analyst can handle whatever disturbances or complications her extra-analytic activities or writings throw into the transference with grace. But I do largely reject Phyllis Greenacre's position. What is required of the analyst in the social—in her writings, in her doings—is not insignificant, but it is I think less on the order of sacrifice and restraint, than of tact. Which is fine by me.

*   *   *

Gunn writes,

> If there's nothing natural about speech in the first place, still less anything natural about analysis or writing, then where does this leave that strange sort of supplement that is writing about analysis? The highly artificial mechanisms are obvious enough when analysts write, since it's so patent that they're doing so under duress, manufacturing

scant scraps of knowledge they can share so as to relieve the diabolical solitude of their profession.

But their patients?

He's not entirely wrong about analysts' writing. But, there are other ways for analysts to write, outside of the place of manufacturing, of scraps, of knowledge. One can emerge as a patient, which is what an analyst always, essentially, must do.

*   *   *

If I were to write out the course of my analysis thus far as a series of signifiers—a kind of private analytic orthography, though I suspect that many if not most analyses could be similarly hieroglyphed—it would look like this:

Bobby boy
Snowman
Frosty
Marmalie
Woodhouse
Snarlag
Fem Sem Es

They're sequential, but with a catch. The first five are from my pre-analytic life—mostly childhood, but also adolescence—and came up and returned at various times throughout my analysis. The last two were produced during my analysis, made in the matrix of the transference. They mark the beginning of my doing the work of conception myself: that is, of my finally accepting the bounty of the unconscious.

This sequence can be mapped onto the other set of signifiers that I will be tracking here, which comprises the titles of many books: *The Double, First Love,* and *The Gift.*

Here is a list of these books. As a compendium of texts, it leaves out such things as films, jazz recordings, folk song collections, motion picture soundtracks, and other productions that also go by the names The Double, First Love, and The Gift. I would hazard that these three titles are those that are distributed among the largest number of cultural artifacts, perhaps because they are signifiers that testify to both specificity and plurality. In other words, they speak to the transcendence of self through the rigor of its articulation. We all know something about each of them: double, first love, gift.

Even so, the list is surely incomplete, as lists always are, at the same time that it loops in on itself, the names of some of these books explicitly referencing some of the others. Thus, these are titles that make manifest the history of transmission, influence, imitation, envy, rivalry, desire, and love that always inheres at the acts of reading and writing. I have not read most of them, but I would like to read some of them, together.

The Double:

Greg Boyd (novel)
Fyodor Dostoevsky (novella)
Otto Rank (psychoanalytic theory)
Jose Saramago (novel)
Don Webb (novel)

First Love:

Wendy Austin (hybrid: personal, scholarship)
Isaac Babel (short story)
Samuel Beckett (short story)
Harold Brodkey (personal essay)
John Clare (poem)
Richard Cumberland (play)
E.M. Delafield (novel)
Maria DiBattista (scholarship)
Elena Garro (novella)
Søren Kierkegaard (hybrid)
Margracia Loudon (novel)
Charles Morgan (novel: renamed, *Portrait in a Mirror*)
Joyce Carol Oates (Gothic tale)
Gwendolyn Riley (novel)
Edwin Rolfe (poetry)
Mikhail Roshchin (novel)
Eugene Scribe (play)
Bethany Strong (novel)
Samuel Taylor (play)
Ivan Turgenev (short story)
Eudora Welty (short story)

The Gift:

Barbara Browning (autofiction, novel)

Helen Coutant (children's book)
David Flusfeder (novel)
Marie Agnes Foley (play)
Martin David (poems)
Peter Dickinson (novel)
Hilda Doolittle (novel)
Hafiz (poetry)
Emyr Humphreys (novel)
Lewis Hyde (scholarship)
Aafke E. Komter (scholarship)
Mary Lumsden (play)
Marcel Mauss (sociological study)
Vladimir Nabokov (novel)
Joan Lowery Nixon (Young Adult fiction)
Florence Noiville (novel)
D. De Warrdenau (poetry)

* * *

It is possible that Double, First Love, and Gift, taken psychoanalytically, also comprise a sequence—that they are a kind of ordering. Of what? Of psychosexual development, with the dyad of the pre-Oedipal period, through Oedipus and first love, and on to some refiguring of these matters at the moment that one both accepts and takes responsibility for the bounty of the unconscious? Of an analysis as it rehearses or makes possible these developments? Of Lacan's career-in-concepts, from the Imaginary of his early thinking, to the Symbolic of the middle of his career, to the Real, to which he devoted his energies at the end, in his work on Joyce and the sinthome (itself a creative construction or artistic act)? Yes and no; or, yes only to the extent that these sequences themselves belie chronology, earlier stages inscribing the germs of the later, later stages activating and reorganizing the earlier. As the coordinates of subjectivity, Imaginary, Symbolic, and Real cannot be extricated one from the other, no matter how you talk about them, or when. If anything, these three sets of titles map the nodal points of an analysis as it gives shape to the subject, and as it is both bound to and undercuts fantasies of development.

Thus Double, First Love, and Gift are literary or cultural figurations of certain Freudian-Lacanian ideas—the uncanny, the mirror stage, Oedipus, sublimation, the sinthome—that are also quilting points in psychoanalytic theory. This book will be a working-through of that theory in real time, at a juncture in my passage from analysand to analyst at which I find it important to register that effort. Psychoanalytic theory takes its place here as a palimpsest of my encounters with foundational texts that have worked on me progressively, and to which I have turned and returned, in various contexts and with various others similarly engaged in the passions of psychoanalysis. Inevitably, there will be misunderstandings and mistakes, in the sense that writing is always in one way or another symptomatic—mistakes and symptoms being, in psychoanalysis, of especial value. In any case I offer these theoretical fragments less as a didactic instrument than as a record of the place of theory in the process of becoming an analyst. I offer them as a way of conjugating literature, theory, and autobiography, with the hazy sense that to do so speaks somehow to both psychoanalysis and to femininity, and to what reading and writing have to do with both.

I would like to evoke something of the course of an, or rather my, analysis—of the play between the specific and the shared, the autobiographical and the theoretical, as psychoanalysis articulates it—by working through these nodal points in psychoanalytic theory, these signifiers, and these literary texts that share their titles. Thus Bobby Boy, Snowman, Marmalie, and Frosty—all figures from my early childhood that testify to my location in the world of semblances—will fall under the category of The Double, along with psychoanalytic theory (Freud on the uncanny, Lacan on the Imaginary) and Dostoevsky's novella. Woodhouse—which refers to the domestic novels and marriage plots that are part of my intellectual heritage—will come in under First Love, alongside psychoanalytic theory on Oedipus and the Symbolic and the texts of Babel and Turgenev. Snarlag and Fem Sem Es then are Gift—which means, they speak to the creative resources of the human person that, without leaving behind entirely the problems of double and first love, are able to organize their effects more workably. They will take their place with psychoanalytic theory about creativity as it negotiates impossibility (sublimation, the sinthome, the Real), Nabokov, and Browning.

As you can see, most of the works of literature that I will be dealing with are from the Russian novelistic canon. Before I started psychoanalytic training, I was a scholar of Russian literature, having pursued a long PhD in the field and taught in it for many years. These are all texts that have lived with me for a very long time, and their centrality to this project is purely personal. And yet, within the personal, structure makes its presence felt. I have argued in various academic articles that the Russian cultural discourse and national fantasy is an hysterical one. Whatever the validity of that claim, clearly I have long identified with Russia and its letters. To write here, for perhaps the last time, about these works of literature that I have been writing about for what feels like forever—to write about them as part of a long-overdue accounting of what they have meant to me—will be my way of saying goodbye to that hysterical identification. It will be a way of marking the passage from the position of the hysteric to that of the analyst—which, as Lacan says, a good analysis must eventually allow you to do.

Chapter 2

THE DOUBLE

Bobby Boy was a doll I named after a boy from the local playground whom I once saw peeing in the bushes, when I was around three. I suppose I was spying on him. I don't remember the scene so much as the feeling afterward, a distress I had not previously known possible. It was the first of many falls. I hadn't known there were those things out there, that some people had and I didn't. (This may be a screen memory.)

I later got a boy doll—or maybe I rechristened one I already had—that had brown hair like playground Bobby. I carried him around for years, stroking his hair between two fingers until one section of it stood straight up in an obscene cowlick. He's still sitting on a shelf in my old bedroom, smiling blankly.

I'm not sure whether Bobby Boy's protruding cowlick was meant to commemorate the realization or the ignorance, the thing itself or the lack of it—probably both. The organ was appropriately displaced to the place of knowledge, coming from the head, which is where, moving forward, I tended more consciously to experience my various strivings and deficiencies. The horror of coming to know I didn't know something was repeated many times over. What got lost is what appeared as a surprise in this writing: the orality of cowlick. I tend to look for salvation in the wrong places, not realizing that the magic I'm seeking is already located elsewhere.

* * *

To Lacan, the human subject, bearer of ego, is constituted as such at the moment (not so much a temporal moment as a logical one) at which it identifies with its own image in the mirror: what he calls, the mirror stage. This is also a moment of naming: "That is you!" It is an instance that marks our self-alienation along the two axes of image and language, a split that makes identity possible; it is associated at once with pleasure (*that* is me? That whole, functioning, competent-seeming person?) and loss (that is *me*?). As Mladen Dolar writes, when I see myself in the mirror "it is already too late. There is a split: I cannot recognize myself and at the same time be one with myself." The appearance of the double in the mirror—as it registers alienation, castration, and death—is our payment for living as ourselves.

But the double also haunts us for that reason, since in producing the split it also commemorates its closure. Freud says that the original double, as a figure in literature and culture, was the soul, the guarantor of immortality; in modern literature, the double has taken on the opposite aspect, as the harbinger of death. This may be only to say that in allowing for life, the double also takes onto itself the power to cause its collapse. Which then is why stories of the double generally end in disaster, since the moment at which you encounter your double—meet him, merge with him, cede your place to him—you are also returned to the logical instance in which, double-less, you do not properly exist.

Dolar writes that the loss that comes with the registration of the double is, on the level of the object, that of Lacan's object *a*, "that part of the loss that one cannot see in the mirror, the part of the subject that has no mirror reflection, the nonspecular." The familiar, sensical, domesticated world only exists as such as a result of the loss or "'falling out'" of this object *a*. Thus objectivity and subjectivity achieve their contours simultaneously with the fall of this object which, as the condition for knowledge and the coherence of imaginary reality, cannot itself be seen or known.

The horror of seeing your double beyond the mirror is that at that moment the subject appears with the object intact. The double is the mirror image that hasn't lost the object. (The double is one's psychosis.) In the mirror, I can see my eyes, but not my gaze which is lost in the constitution of subjectivity. So what if you see your mirror image blink? "That would make the object as gaze appear in the mirror." In stories called *The Double*, the moment that the double makes us know that for him the object is not lost—"a wink or a nod is enough" to convey this—is precisely the moment that everything collapses, and the mutual construction of subjectivity and objectivity fails. "The imaginary starts to coincide with the real, provoking a shattering anxiety" (Dolar).

Barthes talks about the *punctum*, the unassimilable detail in a photograph (say) that pricks the viewer, the traumatic hole or nodal point of the image that, in opening to the abyss, evokes the subject of or as desire. In Lacan this is something like the stain ("la tache") that, as in Holbein's painting *The Ambassadors*—which calls the eye to see a blot in the painting that bears the shape of a skull—reveals to us our own capture by the gaze: the extent to which we are in the painting right at the vanishing point where death emerges. At one point Lacan describes being on a fishing boat and feeling himself watched by the gleam from a sardine can, shining off the water. The gleam situates the subject in the picture, as object of the primordial gaze, subjected, as object, to death. In the act of painting, the painter similarly submits himself to the scopic drive by which he is seen by the things around him, inscribing himself in the picture at the place of the stain that is also the desire and capture and death of the viewer. As Lacan says, "I am photographed." The double then takes its place on this register, since it makes manifest what is usually repressed, that is, the extent to which the drive impinges from outside. The gaze that is mine is also equivalent to my being seen by a look from a hole. Thus the double is, among other things, this very moment at which you see yourself looking at yourself from out there.

In Dostoevsky's *The Double*, the extimacy of the gaze is only just barely repressed from the start. Yakov Petrovich Golyadkin wakes up to a room whose objects "gaze at him familiarly." That's the thing about the domestic: in its very familiarity there is always something lurking. Freud says as much in "The Uncanny," and his is an etymological insight: that the *heimlich*, the comfortable or known or familiar—which also means, of the *heim*, related to the house or the home—coincides at a certain point in the dictionary with the *unheimlich* (the uncanny), precisely to the extent that the home is the definition of the private, hidden, and repressed. The uncanny, as the phenomenon whereby the alien inside enters the scene, constitutes both the opposite of the familiar and the very same thing: *unheimlich* thus makes manifest what is latent in every signifier, that is, that it evokes, is founded on, and represses its own opposite (Saussure; Freud on negation): each word a haunted house, pregnant with the ghost of its mirror image. Every signifier is uncanny. The subject of the unconscious, as it is mapped by language, emerges in those interstices.

Man finds his home at a point located in the Other that lies beyond the image from which we are fashioned. This place represents the absence where we stand. Supposing that, which does indeed happen, it shows itself for what it is—namely, the presence that lies elsewhere, which means that this place is tantamount to an absence—then it becomes the queen of the game, it makes off with the image that underpins it, and the specular image becomes the image of the double, with all the radical uncanniness it brings. (Lacan)

This is all logically true. But does it have to be literally so? Do I really have to find homes—my own, other people's—so profoundly creepy? Whose stuff *is* this, anyway? Why is it looking at me? I was probably drawn to Russian literature because, as Freud says somewhere, the Russians are very close to the unconscious. This is essentialist sure but reading Dostoevsky one does have the sense that there's something to it.

In his seminar on anxiety, Lacan takes it to the letter, and to the grammar, claiming that negation in Russian syntax testifies especially to the dialectic of desire and repression that is the ground of language. In the subjunctive statement, "I fear lest he come" (*je crains qu'il ne vienne*), the signifier of negation ("ne") is "expletive" because it isn't strictly necessary for the conveyance of meaning. Instead, this "ne" is "the signifying trace of what I call the subject of the enunciation," that is, the subject of desire as it speaks through the letter of what is said.

Lacan points out that in the Russian translation of *je crains qu'il ne vienne* (not that he knows Russian—he has spoken with a specialist) there are not one but two expletive morphemes. In other words, when it comes to the signifying traces of desire, Russian doubles it.

*   *   *

Snowman was another early double, though he also had another one. He was a modest creature, forever the sidekick. His partner was Santa Claus, both about two-foot-tall plastic figures that the owners of the deli near our apartment in upper Manhattan, where I lived until age four, put out every winter around Christmas. As I image him up now, I realize that I'm actually picturing Santa Claus, with his red plastic coating and white plastic beard, rather than Snowman himself, who exists in my memory as distinctly less contoured, his whiteness fading into the background, or emerging from it, like a gleam.

I remember vaguely passing by Snowman and Santa Claus with my father on the way to watch Columbia soccer games. For some reason, I pronounced "soccer game," "gammin mamma." I don't believe my mother would attend those games, but apparently I summoned her at them anyway, gaming mommy, playing with the mother's body. If Mom is the one from whom we are sundered by Oedipus, the original other of the dyad, she is also evoked, somehow, by the double. Where is the woman in stories of the double? Always somewhere, never quite there.

Dolar writes that with the entry into the Symbolic that Oedipus marks, the loss at stake in the mirror reflection is shifted onto the Name of the Father, whose law becomes that which refuses the subject his being, as well as his *jouissance* and its primordial object: the mother. "The father takes responsibility for the loss" that already happened; his job is to take onto himself the burden of this exclusion and, in so doing, to make other forms of entry possible. Thus being barred from the woman—from the mother and from the sexual, which also means, barred *by* sexual difference—is a reinscription, at the level of language, of the split that already obtains in the mirror stage.

Evidently Snowman and Santa Claus were imbued with enough anxiety and fascination that they became part of the family mythology. Later, in thinking through why they held such interest, I realized that Santa Claus at least hearkened to a certain obvious exclusion, that is, my exclusion from Christmas (which expulsion itself inscribed a long history of previous ones). We celebrated Hanukkah tepidly, my father's relationship to it weighted by his memories of his father, who successfully fled the Nazis, and my mother's by hers of her atheist, American Communist parents, themselves born of Jews who fled the Pale. Our own Jewishness was ambivalently approached from both directions: as a result both of my father's reaction to his father's single-minded interest in it (in most conversations with the man, you found out about a famous person you hadn't known was Jewish) and of my mother's replication of her parents' rejection of it. We got presents on Hanukkah unaccompanied by any particular ritual.

Stories of doubles are indeed stories of exclusion: from our homes in ourselves by virtue of our existence in the mirror and in language. We can't be in two places at once so we're always not there and we assume other people, with whom we rival as still more doubles, are in that primordially complete place (the unhaunted *heim*) that is properly ours, but lost. This means, in double stories, that the hero's double tends to take his place—in the home, the family, work, and life. This is part of what's at play in racial discrimination.

Evidently though there were other deprivations at stake as well. As a child I pronounced Santa Claus "Ganka Gauze" (like for a wound), and Snowman as "No Man." As though anyone really is.

* * *

Two incredible scenes from *The Double* by Dostoevsky:

> -While speaking to a social superior, Golyadkin lowers his eyes to the ground and notices what seem to be white spots on the latter's boots. "Can they have split open?" he thinks. But no, they are not split: instead, Golyadkin realizes that he is looking at bright reflections

on the surface of the shoes, made of patent leather. "'That's called a *highlight*,'" he thinks. "'The term is used especially in artists' studios; elsewhere this reflection is called a *bright gleam*.'" Then Golyadkin realizes that it's time to speak, and so he says something inane.

-Golyadkin gets to his place of work and his double—a man who is such a complete likeness to Golyadkin that it is impossible to determine "which was the original and which the copy," except that the double talks a lot and Golyadkin doesn't—is already there, preening about. His boss calls to him to bring in a document. He tries to pick up the paper, but his double intervenes. "'And there's a little ink blot here, Yakov Petrovich, have you noticed the ink blot?'" What ink blot?—says Golyadkin. "'I'll just fix it a little, there . . .'" says his double. "'It would be best to remove it with a knife, Yakov Petrovich . . . I'll just use a penknife on it.'" "'My dear sir,'" asks the double, "'do you understand the Russian language?'" Where is the ink blot? There is no ink blot. In the tussle of hands on paper and knives and ink blots seen and unseen and languages spoken and unspoken the double makes away with the document, presents it to the superior, and gets credit for the work.

This is a few pages before the double nods his head, winks his eye, and minces slightly with his feet in the presence of Golyadkin to show him: he most certainly does have *it* (the document, the credit, the woman, the object). And many pages before Golyadkin—having, through the intercession of his double, lost his position at work as well as any hope he had with Klara, his love object—gets carted off to a mental hospital.

Dolar writes that the uncanny is what bars imaginary completion and subjective fulfillment. In double stories, the double intercedes in between the hero and his love object because the uncanny—of which the double is messenger—is a mark of our self-alienation, an ambassador of the unconscious as it registers the impossibility of a return to a primordial unity. The double thus behaves tautologically, since his appearance is the ledger of the impossibility of the sexual relation, which he then proceeds literally to ensure: you can't ever get the girl.

This is all not to mention what else Dostoevsky's scenes offer: the visual register—the reflection, the highlight—as it inscribes a split; the gleam which reveals to the subject his location in the scopic; the ink blot, the knife, the cut, the question of who speaks and who doesn't. Golyadkin's problem is that he doesn't speak and so he is caught in the visual, unable to accommodate its splits. The stain reveals a certain truth, but you can't always see it; it is part of a tug-of-war of imaginary relations, me fighting with my double. Captured by the visual, most of us will continue to fear the knife. We are of course castrated in language as well. But speaking shifts the terms of our relation to this position. If it is heeded, language can move us beyond that capture, as Dostoevsky knows well.

* * *

Frosty was the return of Snowman, or Snowman outlined more explicitly as a double. I think I must have been instructed by my teachers to make my parents a holiday card of some sort, so instead of drawing an elf or snowy tree or dreidel or whatever, I drew a melancholic, white creature—a kind of ambiguous forest animal—standing alone against a white background, gazing out at the viewer. The speech bubble said: "My name is Frosty. There are no other creatures like me, but I am happy." My dad framed the card and put it on his desk in his new office at Amherst College. When I would visit him there, I would stare at it in mute confusion, looking at myself looking back at me in the guise of this cold creature of no particular gender or species.

That I felt I had to assure my parents I was happy is what I now find sad. What I really must have wanted to tell them was, I was freezing. Winters in Amherst were cold and dark. Later, I would develop a symptom where I would get so cold—the damp chill having taken up residence in my bones as insistently as we took up residence in snowy Massachusetts—that I couldn't feel normal again until I took an hour-long hot shower. How perverse that I then went into a field that would require me to be in Russia in the winter. My host families must have hated me for all the hot water I used.

There are no other creatures like me—why would I have thought that? Outside of the human race because I was no man? Because it's chilly to be lacking? If penises go in freezers, and you don't have a penis, then I suppose you must be the freezer. That Frosty was basically a him belies the problem, or at least reveals the contours of my questions about castration while also providing an answer I couldn't see (i.e., that being a him is hardly protection from it). How ridiculous to have encoded a purely aural association—Snowman and no man—on the soma, but so it goes. After a few years of analysis, the symptom disappeared.

In retrospect, I conflate the Frosty card with another drawing I made earlier, shortly after our move to Amherst, as part of an activity at the first birthday party I was invited to in town. It was of me standing on the grass, and the caption read, "This is me, in New York, in the park," but in the creative spelling of a kindergartener. A summer scene rather than a winter one; I suppose I associated the prelapsarian New York days with warmth. It was drawn on one of those Make-A-Plate kits and returned to us, entombed forever in plastic, to sit in the kitchen cabinet as culinary commemoration of whatever it was I was having so much difficulty saying. At some point many years later I realized that I associated my tortuous spelling of "New York" in that caption—two such strange and difficult words, onomatopoeic of the disgust I felt about my childish attachments and movements, ew—with the confusing spelling of "New York" in Russian, as I would learn it much later: the mushy, sticky palatalizations, the complex orthography, with strangely placed soft signs and reversed dipthongs, to account for the foreignness of the city to a Russian speaker. This was a confusion that would never quite leave me in learning Russian: the acute awareness that, like a child, I was an immigrant to the language, and that something of my heritage made me illegible at the same time that the very fact of speaking rendered my actual origins—as New Yorker, as subject—foreign. My problem was that I thought that speaking was my problem—as though any word, or any language, like any city, could be genuinely native.

Or maybe the problem (*why am I always looking for *the problem*?*) was that I *wasn't* an immigrant. God knows my ancestors could speak perfect—perfect!—Russian. Lucky me, to be a native New Yorker. And then, moving from New York to Massachusetts is hardly like fleeing the Nazis, or escaping the Pale of Settlement. But, these things become mythologized, or at least implicitly compared. Identification leads to shame; differentiation, to guilt.

*   *   *

The Double ends with a crowd: Golyadkin among his work associates, who come together to get him taken away by a doctor. "That room, all the rooms—all, all of them were filled to overflowing. There were multitudes of people . . . all . . . clustered around Mr. Golyadkin, all this strained towards Mr. Golyadkin . . . he noticed quite clearly that he was being urged in a certain direction." They are all staring at him and he doesn't understand what they are saying. The doctor has an accent and it does not look promising.

The failure of this book is the failure to take a position within language. Golyadkin is hauled off mutely, never having told his side of things, and the events of the story can be read backward, as an effect of that inability, or refusal. Thus the crowd only serves to usher Golyadkin's final exclusion from his own life, which he would have had to speak his way into, one way or another.

Dostoevsky is known for his collective scenes: people come together from various walks of life, all straining toward something, all desperate to speak. Crazy things happen; there is a lot of shouting; it's all very noisy. These scenes register the problems of communal life; but they also represent the promise held out by language as its medium. Many of Dostoevsky's works end in disaster: the crowd closes in, all of the texts' movement adds up to nothing, and the subject is shut out. Something has gone unsaid. Something is left unaccomplished.

But every once in a while, in Dostoevsky's books, something works. This generally happens when something of the action of the text manages to enact a structural shift such that, instead of shutting down or spinning out, the work's energic force achieves an opening that leads somewhere new. In *The Brothers Karamazov*, this happens, in part, because the Oedipal family with which the novel begins—a disaster of a family, all the women dead, the father a drunkard and lecher, brothers scattered—is by the end of the text reconfigured. By means of a mechanism by which the law is loosened—or, let's say, feminized—the novel's action allows the family to open onto the social: not doing away with genetic families entirely, but massaging their boundaries such that movement within them, and among them, is possible.

People call Dostoevsky a psychological writer; Freud saw him as a precursor. Certainly, Dostoevsky understood something about the unconscious. What is astounding to me is that he understood something specifically about what would become the process of psychoanalysis, and that he encoded this process as a procedure in his texts. In *Crime and Punishment*—like *The Brothers Karamazov*, both a family novel and a police procedural, as family novels often in one way or another are, children generally little criminals and little detectives at once, like Oedipus—what is demanded of Raskolnikov, the murderer, is not doing hard time or repaying his victims or even any kind of obvious social penance, but speech. He must say what he has done: not talk around it, not indicate it gesturally, not wait for other people to guess, which is what he spends most of the book doing. He has to take responsibility for his act, and this means that he has to speak it in its specificity, including by saying the names of his victims. Most readers don't remember the name of the murdered pawnbroker because Raskolnikov rarely speaks it throughout the book, calling her instead, an old crone, a louse, etc.

This act of speech would also mean rectifying the fault that produced the murder, which, as in *The Double*, was a sin not only of silence, but of the gaze. Raskolnikov is unwilling to look at his victim's face. He splits her head in half with an axe as he looks at her scalp, thus projecting outward his rage at his own split self. "Raskol" means "split" in Russian, but that is essentially what every name means. In being named you are made subject to language and the social; in that subjection you are subjectivized, the unconscious is drawn, you are split from yourself, made a creature of desire, which for Dostoevsky also means being a creature of grace and God. The book is filled with dreams. Thus Raskolnikov needs not only to account for himself in language but also to account *for* language and its effects. In implicitly asking Raskolnikov to speak his victims' names, the novel is demanding not that he suture his split—as I think naïve readings of the novel often have it—but that he register that he is not alone in this split state: that is, he must avow his own desire by way of that of the other precisely by speaking their mutually split existence within language.

Most broadly, the text calls on Raskolnikov to speak better, and to see better by speaking better. He can't do it alone. Throughout the book, his partners in this endeavor are Sonya, the saintly prostitute, who knows something about speech and desire; and the policeman, Porfiry Petrovich. It is in *Crime and Punishment* that the action of the Dostoevskian police takes on its most distinctive aspect. Porfiry Petrovich is not much of a detective. He doesn't seem terribly interested in collecting evidence; he doesn't run around tracking anyone down. When Raskolnikov sees him in his office, which he does a few times over the course of the book, he goes of his own volition. What Porfiry Petrovich says to Raskolnikov is enigmatic, but one thing is clear: he is waiting, and he is listening. He wants Raskolnikov to confess. He will wait as long as it takes for Raskolnikov to take responsibility for himself. Sure, he wants eventually to get a guilty verdict—sure, that's what confession manifestly would achieve. Sure, he thinks he's a policeman. But, in the action of the book, he is not a policeman. He is a psychoanalyst.

Dostoevsky wanted to turn the detective novel on its head, to show that law in Russia is conceptually different from the West, that bourgeois discipline, for one, does not obtain there. In the Russian cultural imaginary in Dostoevsky's hands, closure—legal, domestic, narrative—never descends. The novels' legal apparatus is meant not to shut anything down or to lock anyone up, but rather to usher further propulsion. Juridical systems attend to unconscious truth rather than rationalist argumentation and evidentiary material.

I have contended at various times that the Russian national mythology figures Russia as a space of lack, and thus of desire. Especially in nineteenth-century Russian letters, Russia's was a conceptual geography in which the phallic supports of the West—industrial capitalism, Enlightenment empiricism, and rationalism—were absent. Clearly, I was mostly writing autobiography. I lived in Russia after college because I wanted to be in a space of desire, without phallic support. The position I took on was privileged, and problematic: the American tourist dabbling in not-having. But, at the very least, the time I spent there served as a model for what that space might feel like, for whenever I was ready to take it on more seriously. It was my first time being truly alone.

*   *   *

All of this—the function of lack and desire, and also dissatisfaction, in the Russian cultural imaginary; the challenge to the phallic Western masters to whom this mythology is in part addressed; the simultaneous rebellion against and obeisance to authority—means that Dostoevsky, as he gives voice to the Russian cultural positioning in the nineteenth century, writes from the position of the hysteric. He was out to hystericize the novel genre. He is a purveyor of hysterical realism, which means, his is a realism that points to a conversion of reality. This is also the meaning of Christ in his texts. Hysteria as a cultural idea has a complicated history, equally reviled and romanticized. Lacan viewed the discourse and subjective position of hysteria as one turn of the screw away from those of the analyst. As much as the analyst returns to the hysteric her words askew in order to introduce the dimension of cure as it lies in the direction of unconscious desire, the hysteric is already herself just one click away. This is why when an obsessional goes into analysis, he must be hystericized first. Then, analysis can begin.

*   *   *

At the end of *Crime and Punishment*, Raskolnikov says what he has to say, more or less. The logic of the book demands a certain grammar from his confession: subject, verb, object. He needs to say, I killed, and then he needs to speak the names of his victims. He doesn't speak the name of his second victim. This may very well represent the idea that, in psychoanalysis or anywhere, it is impossible to say *it*, to say everything, to speak oneself out. Dostoevsky's poetics are characterized by what Mikhail Bakhtin called this "unfinalizability" of speech: the extent to which, in Lacanian terms, the speaking or desiring subject will always have to keep going and say more. But, at least, at a certain point, it is possible to have said enough. Something having been uttered, in the context of a long chain of words—a long analysis, a long novel—will be sufficient to achieve a structural shift and propel you out of the telling in which you are located. Raskolnikov's confession, incomplete as it is, is this enough. After its utterance, we are shunted out of the novel and into the epilogue, which is a radically different geography and narrative space. We are no longer in St. Petersburg, teeming with crazy people, or in Raskolnikov's head, teeming with crazy thoughts, or in the novel proper as it tracked the traffic between the two. We are in a work camp in Siberia, cold and empty, by a river, in the narrative space not of novel, but of journalism—outside of the fiction, propelled into reality.

Readers have various reactions to the epilogue as it marks a radical change in the novel. I like it, because I think it does two important things. For one, it allows us to watch the escalation of the novel's energies until the moment of confession, at which point, something—though what exactly is unclear—is brought to an end, an opening is achieved, and we are brought someplace radically new. And, it shows us what it looks like to leave a novel and enter real life. In the novel's paradoxical economy, the criminal's arrest is precisely an opening, and it is achieved via the pressure of Raskolnikov's transferences: his forms of love for, and his ways of being loved by, Porfiry Petrovich and Sonya. Moreover, what is required for the intensification of these energies is that the work on Raskolnikov be carried out also by others. By the end of the novel, it is as though everyone and everything in the book, buoyed by Raskolnikov's transferences, has been pushing him toward the moment at which he can change his life. I think there is no better picture than this of the end of an analysis.

Sonya accompanies Raskolnikov to the prison camp. Ever the faithful woman, she is willing to wait as long as it takes for Raskolnikov to get out, without any guarantee that he will. She is the ground on which his cure will be effected. With Dostoevsky, we are not meant to question self-sacrifice, or waiting; his ethic is, you wait as long as it takes for grace to come, even if it never does. Psychoanalysis does take a lot of patience, and waiting: breakthroughs come slowly. But, if it does its work, it can allow you to stop waiting for your life to begin.

And so what, finally, of Sonya? Where is her analyst; where is her life? She has supported her family members in one way or another forever. What if there's more that she wants to do? What if she wants to be alone?

*   *   *

Lacan writes of Freud's dream of Irma's injection, that it ends in a crowd. At the moment of facing something like the Real of Irma's mouth— her body, her cavity, her recalcitrance, her drive—Freud's ego, as such, disappears, and he is left with its constituent identifications, who take over in the dream (Dr. M, Otto, etc.). Lacan says that throughout his study of dreams, Freud repeatedly hits a moment where he says, "*I'm not in the dream where one might think.*" There is always a moment at which I disappear—at which I am absorbed into my identifications— and in my very occlusion, I am dispersed. This is something like the baring of the function of the ego, where its splintering on the imaginary register, far from indicating a regression—Lacan says, this is not about the stages of ego development, as the ego psychologists would have it— instead opens up the emergence of the function of the Symbolic, and points to the work of the unconscious as such:

> If there is an image which could represent for us the Freudian notion of the unconscious, it is indeed that of the acephalic subject, of a subject who no longer has an *ego*. And yet he is the subject who speaks, for that's who gives all the characters in the dream their nonsensical lines—which precisely derive their meaning from their nonsensical character.

This moment at which "the discourse of the multiple *ego* makes itself heard in a great cacophony" is I think what Dostoevsky, whose writing is so akin to dreaming, is evoking in his crowd scenes: everyone shouting, the subject lost in the din, surrounded by characters with nonsensical lines, nowhere to be seen and yet everywhere at once.

*   *   *

Freud thought that self-sacrifice should be questioned. With the hysteric, for example—with Dora—the analyst must eventually question her forms of self-sacrifice in order bring into play the matter of what she wants. Probably, Dostoevsky's distance from this position is part of what peeved Freud about the Russian writer, whom he read, and thought about, and criticized for his religious pietics and ideological obeisance to the Russian tsar. To Freud, these failings were elements of Dostoevsky's unanalyzed hysteria, which included as a symptom the writer's famous epileptic fits. Freud says that Dostoevsky, with his artistic genius and ethical seriousness, could have been "the liberator of humanity." Instead, in his neurosis—neurosis always being a prison cell of one's own making—"he appointed himself its gaoler."

I have never much liked "Dostoevsky and Parricide." It shows both Dostoevsky and Freud at their worst. Freud is in certain ways right about Dostoevsky's writings. They are neurotic, and the position on which his most successful works land—such as the collective harmony that, in *The Brothers Karamazov*, is made possible by a return to the maternal embrace, which is in turn the novel's figuration of Christian love—is nothing if not regressive. Freud gives as the definition of "holy," "something based on the fact that human beings, for the benefit of the larger community, have sacrificed a portion of their sexual liberty"—specifically, the freedom to commit incest. Easier to view mommies as the bearers of communal utopias. In any case, it's true that utopian fantasies don't really get you very far.

Freud's skepticism is hard to argue with. And yet, why would he insist on such fault-finding—which makes him at times an ungenerous reader—if he wasn't acting out one of his own neurotic failings, that is, his jealousy?

*   *   *

"The Uncanny" begins with Freud's admission that he doesn't know much about the subject: he is not prone to the uncanny feeling. He is also not prone, apparently, to writing about art and literature, since "it is only rarely that a psychoanalyst feels impelled to investigate the subject of aesthetics." Except, all the evidence speaks to the contrary: writings on Dostoevsky, on Leonardo, on Jensen's "Gradiva," on Michelangelo's *Moses*, on *Hamlet*, *The Merchant of Venice*, *King Lear*, and *Macbeth*, on Goethe's *Dichtung und Wahrheit*, on fairy tales, on mythology, and, in "The Uncanny," on E. T. A. Hoffman's "The Sand Man." So why, in "The Uncanny," in which the uncanny feeling and the aesthetic are so closely aligned, does Freud exclude himself from both?

Out of jealousy, for one. Freud is jealous of creative writers. In "The Uncanny," literature asserts its predominance over "real life"—the material of the psychoanalyst—precisely because it is a "much more fertile province" for the uncanny. Dolar says that in his investigation of the uncanny, Freud uses basically the whole kit and caboodle of psychoanalytic concepts: "Castration complex, Oedipus, (primary) narcissism, compulsion to repeat, death drive, repression, anxiety, psychosis, etc.," such that the uncanny becomes "the pivotal point around which psychoanalytic concepts revolve." But the uncanny is also a pivot in the competition between the creative writer and the psychoanalyst, and thus, in serving as a nodal point in psychoanalysis, the uncanny also testifies to its imagined limits. The mirror stage, as the place of imaginary identifications—which are all in one way or another illusory—is also the place of rivalry, competition, aggression, revenge.

What is at stake for Freud here is less the matter of "real life" versus fiction, than of forms of writing. The uncanny is the province of literature because the creative writer has the license to represent the world as he pleases. "We accept his ruling in every case," and in fact, we react to his creations as though they were real. "By the time we have seen through his trick it is already too late and the author has achieved his object"—the creation of the uncanny feeling—often by bringing in supernatural elements. In these ways, "The story teller has a *peculiarly* directive power over us."

It's not hard to see why Freud might be envious. It can be tedious to explain, to convince, to revise, to prove. Freud is at his worst when he gets argumentative with his reader: I know you will doubt me, I know you don't believe me, I can't give all the details, it's hard to explain to someone who's never been in analysis! I know you want to hate what I'm saying, but look into your own hearts; don't you see that you hate me because you know that I'm right? That you hate me when I speak of sex and sexual repression because in your sexual life, too, something is awry? That you hate me when I say that neurotic illness is a form of not wanting to know about the unconscious because you, too, don't want to know about it? Don't you see that the unconscious is magic, that I can do magic tricks, and that if you listen to me, you will be able to do magic tricks too?

I would wager that these are never productive maneuvers; Freud convinces readers, if he does, despite, not because of, these expository gestures. But you can see why he might be driven to them. How is it possible to say what needs to be said   to satisfy one's own narcissism, but also because what you have to say might make possible the alleviation of suffering—to people who often can't listen because of the very forms of suffering of which you are speaking? It's a paradoxical position that becomes compounded by what is so frequently and understandably the response to its articulation: yeah, Freud, I think you're wrong because you're right? Screw you.

There may be no way out of this battle in the field of writing. Books about Freud the sham, the cocaine addict, the liar, the sex-obsessed megalomaniac, the tyrant of meaning will never stop being published. How fun it must be to write in bold letters, Freud Was Wrong. Probably, one of Freud's faults as both a thinker and a writer was that he couldn't come to terms with that fate—that he was too concerned with being right. This self-positioning—protective, aggressive—may have determined his blind spots as much as anything else. Sure, he was wrong, about lots of things, sometimes grossly, offensively so. But at all times—and this is where his revolution of mind lies—he was speaking of the unconscious: the first to give it a name, to make it the proper object of study and of practice, and to speak of the possibility of the alleviation of suffering not against it, but through it.

* * *

Freud may have been a little sheepish about his disquisition on creative writing in "The Uncanny." At a certain point he bobs his head up and admits, "We have drifted into this field of research half involuntarily." It wasn't quite what he had intended. This claim is reminiscent of his description of repeatedly and involuntarily drifting to a square that housed "painted women," while visiting a provincial town in Italy. He kept losing his way and ending up exactly where he had begun. This, as he describes it, was one of the few situations in his life in which he experienced the uncanny feeling. (The other occurred on a train, when he glimpsed himself in a window and failed to recognize the old man in the reflection.)

The coordinates here are all sketched: the uncanny; the aesthetic, literature, and writing; and the feminine. The uncanny maps the action of a repetitive, involuntary return to the fertile provinces of both the feminine and the aesthetic, which may be codes for each other (painted/women). Freud spends much of "The Uncanny" linking the uncanny feeling with castration: much as he returns to the painted women and to literature, he comes again and again to the anxiety associated with the castration complex as the prime cause of the uncanny effect in "The Sandman" and, by implication, in other stories, and in real life. Is this because castration is the bedrock of psychoanalysis, of the unconscious? (As Freud says, every analysis runs up against castration as a gravitational center; this is the neurotic's ultimate impasse.) Or, is it because castration, in this essay, is the bedrock of writing?

Hélène Cixous claims that Freud's hypothesis that castration anxiety lies at the heart of the uncanny is an effect more than anything of his position as a writer, since without this potential solution, "the narration would be castrated." Thus, "The fear of castration comes to the rescue of the fear of castration." Through the thesis of castration anxiety, Freud asserts his mastery over his text; in so doing, he stakes his place against the creative writers that, throughout the essay, he seems to envy for their ability to do without his own tactics of proof and explanation, and who are associated with painted women as emissaries of the aesthetic. Thus Freud's self-exclusion from both the uncanny and the aesthetic is part of a struggle with femininity—itself bound up with a refusal of writerly castration, which he both maintains and regrets. What if he could have been more like those creative writers, without the need for phallic support? What if he could have left a gap in his logic, a mystery, a beautiful veil, an unanswered question? He might have taken a lesson here from his dream of Irma. But he doesn't, and this means that, in "The Uncanny," Freud mistakes something of his subject, as though he could only be lured into the dislocations of the uncanny while away from the space that is its proper location—to the extent that in both of the instances of the uncanny in which Freud includes himself in the essay, he is away from home. He more than anyone should know that if the home is also the un-home, then one need not wait for a vacation to send a dispatch from the uncanny. There is something here that is keeping Freud from properly locating himself in the scene of his own writing.

Yet castration is also the bedrock of writing because "at the end of the day," as Lacan says, "castration is none other than the moment of interpreting castration." For Lacan, the neurotic turns away not from castration, "but from turning his castration into what the Other lacks. He shrinks back from turning his castration into something positive, namely, the guarantee of the function of the Other." Castration is the wedding ring of our marriage to the Symbolic and to language. It is what provokes us to write, to interpret, to research, to speak—if you're not missing something, why do any of these things?

*   *   *

In "The Sandman," Nathaniel, the central character, starts off the story as a writer. We first hear his voice in a letter to his friend Lothaire, the brother of his love object Clara. (Dostoevsky named Klara in *The Double* after Hoffmann's.) The letter is about his childhood; it mentions

Clara and then is sent to her by accident. She writes back, knowing full well that there is meaning in mistakes.

Nathaniel presents himself as a case history in madness. As he tells it, the primal scene occurs when, as a child, he sneaks into the study to spy on his father and Coppelius, a strange lawyer, both half-undressed, as they work on something ghastly. What can be born of two men? Nathaniel is a writer because writing is a way to produce without the help of a woman. All you need is two men writing back and forth: you and your friend, you and you. And yet, there Clara is, reading the letter that was of course meant for her eyes in the first place, if only so that Nathaniel can be sure that she has witnessed her own elision. This insistence then registers its own impossibility, since in this economy it is Clara who stands in the way of Nathaniel's commune with himself. The double may bar our return to a primordial unity represented by boy gets girl; but the girl is also the double of the double, upsetting the mirror play between boy and boy, at once destination and interference. In this sense Clara takes up the place of language itself, which Nathaniel, try as he might, cannot control. Probably writers are writers because they are desperate to do so but of course they fail from the start.

In "The Sandman," the whole mess actually starts with language and women, and a confusion of tongues among them. Whenever Coppelius comes to visit Nathaniel's father, his mother tells him to go to bed because the Sandman is coming. But when he asks who the Sandman is she says, there is no Sandman—I just mean that you are tired, rubbing your eyes, as though you had sand in them. Later Nathaniel asks his sister's nurse the same question, and she says, oh yes, the Sandman is a wicked man who comes when children won't go to bed, throws sand in their eyes, removes the eyes from their sockets, and feeds them to his bird-children, who use their beaks also to remove eyes from the heads of naughty kids.

How could Nathaniel not be confused? One woman says that the Sandman is coming though he doesn't exist. It was a metaphor. And yet, someone really is coming—the mystery persists—Nathaniel's first attempt at research is left unsatisfied. So, he pursues another source, who confirms Nathaniel's sense that the Sandman is hardly a trope. And yet, the nurse's story also contradicts that reality, since whenever this someone comes, Nathaniel is already in bed. Why would the Sandman, who comes when children won't go to bed, show up when I'm already tucked in? For that matter, why would the Sandman steal children's eyes to feed to his own kids when they are already perfectly well equipped to peck out eyes for themselves? All of the terms of all of these accounts contradict each other, and themselves.

Thus the scene between Coppelius and the father is a primal scene not only because of its structure and imagery, but also because it takes place in the context of Nathaniel's search for knowledge about what goes on in the dark corners of the domestic space; because it expresses the phantasmatic contours of the child's questions (who has what, who takes what from whom, and who does violence to whom); and because it speaks to the impossibility of what that research pursues. The primal scene is the sign of origin that cannot itself be signaled, the germ of narrative that is extimate to the tale, structuring the border. The uncanny as it is produced by the domestic testifies to the emergence of this horrific reality: mom and dad do it. Everything looks nice and neat and homey, the cupboards are well stocked, the china is chipless, my toys are arranged, but there is something else that happens here. Stories are told around this scene, metaphors are produced, but they don't make sense. There is no amount of language or framing that can account for what is happening. One has to see it for oneself.

*   *   *

In Lacanian terms, the familiar may be considered the register of demand. Demand gives an image or object to the constitutive lack in all of us: I want something, but what is it? Do something for me, get me something to answer this want! Buy me flowers, get me an anniversary gift, do the dishes, don't forget the milk! You got the wrong kind, why do you always get the wrong kind, why don't you remember which kind I like? Why are your socks always on the floor, why do you leave the lights on, don't you know by now which one is for paper and which for plastic? To Lacan, neurotics function on the register of demand because they have trouble with the desire that is the proper corollary of lack. Instead of moving within lack, the neurotic produces demands by which that lack is hastily, domestically filled. There is stasis in this. Demand, which is the activity so often of the family, and of the house with its many accoutrements. It's so familiar you could spend your whole life with it. But as Cixous says, the "insistence of the familiar gives rise to what is uncanny, in the long run."

*   *   *

The only time Clara takes up the pen in "The Sandman" is to write the letter to Nathaniel. At first, she writes that she is much shaken by what sounds like the reality of his story. And yet, by the end of the letter, she is entreating Nathaniel to exorcise Coppelius, whom she has come to understand as his own figment.

"If there is a dark and hostile power, laying its treacherous toils within us, by which it holds us fast and draws us along the path of peril and destruction, which we should not otherwise have trod; if, I say there is such a power, it must form itself inside us and out of ourselves, indeed; it must become identical with ourselves."

"Be convinced that these strange fears have no power over you, and that it is only a belief in their hostile influence that can make them hostile in reality."

"I am not afraid of [Coppelius] and his disgusting hands."

Evidently it is through the process of writing that Clara comes to see that neither Nathaniel's phantasms nor his pen can hold any power over her.

Nathaniel and Clara have been a pair since they were basically children. She is a doting companion. "Clara was attached to her lover with all her heart, and when he parted from her the first cloud passed over her life. With what delight, therefore, did she rush into his arms when, as he had promised in his last letter to Lothaire, he actually returned to his native town and entered his mother's room!" A sweet, homey affair. And yet, what are all these other people doing there, at the scene of the lovers' reunion? Nathaniel's incestuous tie to his mother has been commented on frequently by readers of the story; the homoerotic bond between Nathaniel and Lothaire is pretty clear. But what about Clara's strange tie with her brother, who is always by her side, who rescues her gallantly when Nathaniel goes mad and tries to throw her off a cliff, and who seems content to play his part in a threesome with his sister? For that matter, what do we make of the plan, hatched while things are looking up, that Nathaniel, Clara, Lothaire, and Nathaniel's mother all move into a charming little hut together? Do we really believe that "the first cloud" that passed over Clara's life occurred when *Nathaniel* left her? She's an orphan! God knows what she has transferred onto him. And what was Clara doing in Nathaniel's mother's room in the first place when he arrives back from his travels? This is a very sick family, and if the history of sexuality and its repressions is in part what comes to light in the moment of the uncanny, it's no wonder Nathaniel goes nuts. The question is: Why is everyone, Clara included, so convinced that Clara is so sane?

As Dolar writes, the figure of the automaton, the exemplary listener who mostly only says "Ah!" and "Oh?," is "the character exploited by the position of the analyst," such that Nathaniel's conversations with Olympia—the robot he falls in love with in a twist as weird as the rest of the story—"prefigure the analytic session." The analyst as automaton puts on stage the patient's own automatism, that is, her symptom as a form of mechanical repetition, thus provoking the mechanism of repetition in order to work it through.

Aside from Olympia, there are two other figures of the psychoanalyst in "The Sandman"—two characters who listen to Nathaniel, take his troubles seriously, but also maintain that they are in his head: Clara, and Nathaniel's friend named, uncannily enough, Siegmund. Clara and Siegmund are not swayed by Nathaniel's ravings; they are, as Nathaniel shouts at Siegmund at one point, "cold, prosaic fellows." Clearly, Freud wrote about "The Sandman" in part because he saw himself and many of his own questions in it; Nathaniel's accusation to Siegmund echoes Freud's claims about his own immunity to the uncanny feeling. And yet, one wonders why Freud would consign himself to being a "cold, prosaic fellow." In other words, why would Freud take the story at face value; why would he insist that analysts themselves neither experience the uncanny feeling nor produce it in their writings? Just because you play the automaton in session doesn't mean you are one in real life. If the uncanny is code for the emergence of the unconscious as a register of castration, then surely psychoanalysts are privy to it—that's the point. Something of Freud's trouble with castration is running interference in his reading, precisely around the question of the analytic position as the story evokes it, and as it is bound up with femininity, and loss.

Cixous points out that, as representatives of the *heimlich* in "The Sandman," Clara and her brother are "attenuate[d] . . . to the point of effacement" in Freud's essay, with Freud repeating Nathaniel's gesture of eliding the centrality of the woman. But perhaps more to the point is that, in serving as representatives of the *heimlich*, Clara and Lothaire also necessarily represents the *unheimlich* as well, to which their peculiar relationship attests. This may determine Freud's elision as much as anything else. One might have expected him to put Clara to question, ending the story as she does absolutely couched in the domestic, with a husband at her side and two sons at her feet, having given up doing any writing—since why write from within such bliss? She has it all: the phallic mother. How nice to imagine one. It is here that castration anxiety and marriage trouble intersect, since in taking the story's word for it on the register of loss, Freud also takes the story's word for it on the register of marriage: Clara's domesticity knows no return of the repressed. And this is in part because, in order to interrogate Clara's domestic tableau on the register of the uncanny, one would have to resist the marriage plot as the story installs it, which might also mean interrogating one's own relationship to domesticity, marriage, and the image of the happy family—perhaps even to love triangles with one's spouse's sibling (in which Freud is rumored to have engaged). It would mean entertaining the possibility that one's own family is a little sick. Such gestures would then be acts of feminine resistance as Felman identifies it—by which we heed both the forms of resistance present in the text and the call to interpellate ourselves in the scene of our reading and writing—and, in this instance, Freud does not perform them.

To Derrida, further, one element of the scene of writing is a writing of oneself through one's proper name, which, for Freud, if he had engaged it, might have meant an interrogation of his name's inevitable binding up with its own negative in the field of marriage: that is, "in Freud und Leid," or, "for better or worse." Plenty of people have criticized Freud's reading of Hoffmann's story and, though I'm loathe to jump on the bandwagon, I am interested in *why* his reading falters; and though this is purely speculative and admittedly wild, what I'm suggesting is that it is because, perhaps for defensive reasons having to do with his own deeply inscribed relationship to marriage vows, femininity, domesticity, and eros, he does not install himself in his writing and reading. This is not to knock Freud too much, since though he explicitly excludes himself from the scene of "The Uncanny," he was also, in other places—places at which he was distinctively attentive to feminine resistance and its fertility—a marvelous self-reader and self-writer whose autobiographical writing, as Derrida says, birthed psychoanalysis.

*   *   *

Marmalie was a stuffed elephant that I got after we moved to Amherst, where my father was to work as the Dean of Students at Amherst College for thirty years. Somehow, as a child, I always thought the title "dean of students" sounded dirty, or a little illicit. There was something mushy and uncouth about the word "dean." Like a kernel you find somewhere that it shouldn't be, moistened by misplacement. Presumably it represented a question that I maintained about my new home, the place that would become so very familiar.

I was with my mother and her mother at a Macy's in the mall. Maybe it was shortly after my grandparents moved to Amherst from New York to join us. My brother must have been with us, but I don't remember him—he is in fact elided from many of my childhood memories, or present only as a vague, strange sensation. When he was born, I didn't take him on as my baby, the way many older children do. I still regret this. Perhaps that day in Macy's I was in search of a baby that I could take on, without feeling I was losing so much.

As I remember it, the store that day—it must have been close to Valentine's Day—was teeming with gray stuffed elephants with red hearts on their chests. Probably there was a group of them on display at the front of the store, but mostly what they represent in my memory are not the replications of late capitalism but a feeling of plenitude. The elephants were made to sit up, and their arms were splayed open to reveal the hearts in a posture that, much later, I would recognize, in a strange visit to a Unitarian church (I was about to start analysis, and was just beginning to have the inkling of wanting a baby, and was looking for something that I couldn't identify) in the figure of Christ. Within the mass (at Macy's, not church), I located the one that was mine: the one that, throughout his time with me—he lived on my bed until the month before I gave birth to my older son, at which point I transitioned him to the bookshelf for a few years before that son took him on as his own—would continue to testify to abundance in the face of (Oedipal, capitalist, domestic) repetition. By the time we got home, I had named him Marmalie.

Winnicott, via Bechdel: "The name given by the infant to these earliest objects is often significant, and it usually has a word used by the adults partly incorporated in it."

Marmalie: when my analyst first slowed down the name for me into its component parts—Marm-a-lie –I heard the questions about sexuation and femininity that Bobby Boy and No Man also posed. I heard as well the missing "school" in the name, "marm" referring both to my relationship to gender and to the academy. Campuses were always my ambivalent home, my family a collection of deans and students, professors all around. That "marm" was a "lie" was then the key I had long been unable to hear, since it took me a very long time to realize that my proper interest was in erotics, not academics.

What I am only now coming to realize is the extent to which the signifier Marmalie encodes perfectly the meeting of specificity and generality on which psychoanalysis balances. I was interested in erotics, not academics—fine, that was me. And yet, academics are always erotics by another name, since adult research carries something of an early epistemophilic passion or infantile sexual curiosity. And as Joan Rivière says, femininity is itself a masquerade, a kind of lie. I say this with all possible affection for lying, which can come close to the truth.

In that truth, there are new possibilities. Bobby Boy and Snowman were cribbed names, stolen from people or things with which I identified and that I envied, images within the visual field. Marmalie—as much as he was a vision of wholeness or no loss, open arms and another trunk protruding from the head, an intellectual phallic mother—was my linguistic invention.

We all have, within us, a store—vast and sprawling, like Macy's—of language. Its elements are shared, imposed, public property; but they are also private, and specific. In this sense each word that we speak both is and isn't a neologism. Marmalie proceeded from me, but his component morphemes preceded me; garden variety nouns and verbs are received from elsewhere but always take on the particular hues and flavors of their speaker. A psychoanalyst's job is to receive the speech that the analysand produces, to register its components in all their specificity—to join in the storing, to move the store—and, when the time is right, to give them back such that they become what, in their profound specificity, they properly are. As much as Marmalie was my mirror image in the form of a gray stuffed elephant staring back at me, he in his naming also prefigured this vocation.

Chapter 3

FIRST LOVE

Woodhouse is the last name of Jane Austen's eponymous heroine in her novel, *Emma*.

The story of my naming goes like this: my father wanted me to be named Emily, my mother wanted me to be named Anna, so they met in the middle at Emma, at which point they realized that I could be named after the Jane Austen novel. Thus literature comes in to represent both the impasse of the sexual relation and its provisional patching up—which is also, in a sense, what it means to have a baby.

I learned later that my maternal grandmother used to reread the entirety of Austen's canon—all of those romances and marriage plots—nearly every year of her adult life. She had a long marriage to a man, my grandfather, whom she clearly found fairly ridiculous; evidently, she told my mother at some point that she would have divorced him had she had any resources of her own. She had gone to college for a couple of years but had to quit when her father got sick; she never worked. She died of a stroke while screaming at my grandfather that everything was his fault.

Literature was my first intellectual love. Particularly novels. There was something familiar about their rhythm: novels are playing the long game, like analyses. Like me. They start out with a problem. (Randal Jarrell: "The novel is a prose narrative of some length that has something wrong with it.") They are symptomatic. They have made a choice—a choice of malaise, a choice of neurosis—the limits of which they are interested in testing. Unhappy families, dirty cities, debts, murders, what-have-you. Mysteries that tend to be explicitly Oedipal, detection the work of the child passionate for knowledge as much as of the policing authorities charged with enacting it. They start with a problem, which they begin by articulating in whatever way they choose, or whatever way they can ("what brought you here?"). They then proceed by working through the store of signifiers implied by that beginning, not until something is resolved, but until something has run its course.

Obviously I'm talking mostly about the nineteenth-century novel, but I'm of the camp that thinks that that was when the genre was, if not exactly born, then at least imbued with its stakes, limits, and desires. The nineteenth century in Europe is the moment that capitalism and the bourgeois, nuclear family imbricate themselves in a way that both calls for narration and makes enactment inevitable. Thus these novels both give voice to the problems of repetition and, in their very status as objects of industrial replication, embody them—like an hysteric. This interest in the interchanges of subjectivity and objectivity then has something to do with their investment in women; in gender and sexuality; in pleasure.

Indeed the formal rhythm of the novel hinges not only on patience (what are novels waiting for, that they take so long to get through?) but also, often, on the structural alternations that get you to whatever discharge the ending seeks. Charles Dickens's *Bleak House* perhaps does it most obviously: narrow, first-person narration alternating with chapters outlining a broader, more abstracted vision of the community. Contraction and dilation. I remember once describing to a group of professors my sense that teaching literature involved elaborating, in the classroom, a rhythm of focus and release, with periods of concentrated close reading succeeded by more explosive conversation. At the time I was faintly aware that I was also talking about the cadence of novels as I understood and enjoyed it. Only in retrospect did I think in horror— my God, was I just talking to those people about orgasms?

"Emma Woodhouse, handsome, clever, and rich." So begins Austen's novel with its many ironies. Emma is the girl who has it all, who wants for nothing—unlike, for example, the Bennet sisters of *Pride and Prejudice*, who, deprived of their paternal inheritance due to an unfortunate legal technicality, exist on the brink of ruin. But the ethics and the aesthetics are the same, Emma's counterintuitive, the Bennets' overdetermined: whatever her fortune, a single woman is virtually by definition in a profound state of want, and it is this vacuity that produces the narrative that will eventually fill it with a husband and a home. And oh will we enjoy the filling, the pleasures of reading—reading as libidinal waiting game for the meaning that comes at the end of a sentence, paragraph, book—compounded by the erotics of the courtship plot. A girl does love a romance novel.

But Austen's is a vicious irony, turning in on itself many times over. Not only do Emma's various advantages belie a want that she must be schooled to recognize, but that schooling also misses the point. The second you give a girl what she wants—or what she says she wants, or what she is told she wants, or what she wants as a function of another's desire—it turns out she wants something else. This something else is originary—Emma calls Mr. Knightley, whose brother is her sister's husband, her "brother" up until they marry—but it is also radically elusive, because it is lost.

Yet the metonymy of desire is one thing; the disciplinary operation of the Victorian marriage plot another. You don't have to look too hard to see its fulfillments as seemly versions of the rape—Clarissa's—on which the English novel was founded. As with most institutions, marriage, especially when it is positioned as telos, misrecognizes something about desire. The register of incest then exists somewhere in between desire as structure of subjectivity and as subject of social restriction. The incest taboo institutes desire as much as object *a* and the phallus both, in their own way, embody or represent it (as Lacan says, desire *is* law; the incest taboo is the law of castration, of desire), and certainly the Victorians knew a great deal about the pulsations of delight that emerge from prohibition. But they also, especially with respect to women, take it a bit too far. This isn't to say that novels necessarily have to be about industrial capitalism, or the institutional miseries of the bourgeois nuclear family, or Oedipus, or the rape of women—at least, I hope not. Maybe that's my question.

I did indeed grow up in a wood house, after we moved from New York when I was four—smack dab in the middle of Oedipus, just weeks after my brother was born. Knightley's sumptuous estate closes in on Emma, eros contained in its walls, among its objects. In *Pride and Prejudice*, Elizabeth Bennet, who goes off the beaten path, tromps through the mud and gets her clothes all dirty, becomes similarly, by the end of the book, the mistress of a well-appointed villa. Readers who are relieved by the secured closures of the marriage plot must also on some level find this troublesome.

Thus my family's move from the apartment to the wood house encoded for me something very profound about my expectations regarding love and its relationship to domesticity, desire and its objects, and containment—the very subjects of my passionate reading over the next several decades.

* * *

It is interesting to see how the dialectic of movement and stasis is encoded in a family's possessions. Growing up, it seemed that our things circulated constantly. Something old would be replaced by something new, something with the allure of the simultaneously alien and familiar. The old would be moved to the attic, which became a kind of a spiderwebbed department store: sundry items on offer, find what you want, you can have it, it's extra, but also saved, remainder retained.

Like her mother before her, my mother has beautiful taste. My mother and grandmother shared a passion for antique Shaker things, which meant the new was always bound up in the old, our house filled with the histories of other families, my brother and I playing among the beautiful ruins. She collected antique spoons with our names engraved on them. A displayed panoply of silver Emma's, are these me or not-me, to whom do those names refer? Daughters and sons to put in your mouth.

But some of these items also spoke the history of our familial inheritance. Thus in my family, as the generations cycle, they also come to rehearse this circulation of objects, the next generation the attic of the first, or the temporary storage place for used things. My grandmother hands down to my mother the artifices of their first home which become the foundation of the next, repurposed to account for psychosexual development—my mother's childhood bed now in the guest room. Things that as a child belonged to adults now belong to you once you're an adult or something like it, every generation just one guestroom off from the last: your childhood a permanent guest in your house.

Mostly, in the traffic between my grandmother and my mother, I think of containers. The most imposing item in my parents' house is an enormous apothecary chest with something like one hundred small drawers, inherited from my grandparents. One hundred small drawers to house banal household items—paperclips or stamps or lace doilies or ribbon—or phantasmatic part-objects: breasts or eyeballs or toenails or teeth. When my sons visit they open and close the drawers in illicit fascination, playing with their grandmother's body. There are always more orifices to discover in my mother's house, more containers to stick your hand in, more ornaments to eye, more sweets to sneak, more precious things to pilfer. You never know what you'll get, though in one drawer of the apothecary is a map that provides the contents of each of the drawers, and whose placement enacts a comic paradox: in encountering the enormous structure, how can you find the map? You would need a map for the map, but where to put it? Inside another apothecary? Chests within chests, apothecaries in apothecaries, all the way down, to nothing. What's more, is the map on the map? Such that when you look at the map, you are seeing a representation that you would have to have already consulted in order to find in order to consult? The mother's body: you can't get in unless you're already in. Infinite regress of symbolic and real.

When my grandmother died my mother cleaned out her closet, which turned out to be filled with boxes and boxes of beautiful shoes and clothes—some designer, some handmade—meticulously labeled with sizes and brand names. I never saw her wear any of them, since she spent most of the time I knew her unimposingly outfitted, shuttling back and forth between home and doctors' offices. What is it about our bodies that we have such trouble knowing, such that knowledge is so needed, such that we take such satisfaction in these maps and lists? I have inherited this penchant for insistent containment and my husband sometimes jokes, maybe we should just put our whole apartment in a huge Tupperware.

* * *

apothecary (n.)

mid-14c., "shopkeeper," especially "pharmacist; one who stores, compounds, and sells medicaments," from Old French apotecaire (13c., Modern French apothicaire), from Late Latin apothecarius "storekeeper," from Latin apotheca "storehouse," from Greek apotheke "barn, storehouse," literally "a place where things are put away," from apo "away" (see apo-) + theke "receptacle," from suffixed form of PIE root *dhe- "to set, put."

The same Latin word produced French boutique, Spanish bodega, German Apotheke. Cognate compounds produced Sanskrit apadha- "concealment," Old Persian apadana- "palace."

Drugs and herbs being among the chief items of non-perishable goods, the meaning narrowed 17c. to "druggist" (the Apothecaries' Company of London separated from the Grocers' in 1617). Apothecaries were notorious for "the assumed gravity and affectation of knowledge generally put on by the gentlemen of this profession, who are commonly as superficial in their learning as they are pedantic in their language" [Francis Grose, "A Classical Dictionary of the Vulgar Tongue," 1796].

Apothecary: the place where inheritance, domesticity, and object life meet the hysteric with her relation to the body; to repression and containment; to pedantic doctors, the masters we seek and revile at one and the same time.

* * *

Freud delineates his main ideas about the Oedipus complex in a couple of very strange essays. "Some Psychical Consequences of the Anatomical Distinction Between the Sexes" makes its subject clear: not only are sexual difference and its discovery central to the Oedipus complex, but they also determine the contours of the Oedipus complex as it traverses differently the lives of boys and girls. The essay centers on castration, that is, on the ways and moments in which boys and girls register sexual difference, as well as on how those registrations affect the course of their erotic and psychic lives. Thus the object of investigation in the essay—the anatomical distinction between the sexes—is also that of the very first investigation of the child, the foundational act of research as it will reverberate in all future researches. Become an astrophysicist, if you like, or a literary scholar, or a philosopher, but each pursuit bears the traces of that initial passion. Show me yours, I'll show you mine. Freud's revolution was in part to continue to pursue those very first objects of infantile research for his whole life.

"The Dissolution of the Oedipus Complex," on the other hand, takes as its subject the overcoming of Oedipus, with the understanding that the possibility and mechanisms of the end of the complex reflect its internal coherence. Thus the coordinates of the essays are beginnings and endings: how Oedipus is initiated, how he is destroyed, and what castration has to do with both of those logical instances. On both poles, girls and boys behave absolutely differently. On both poles, there is nothing that even approaches symmetry.

Freud says that for little boys, it goes like this. Little boys love their mothers because . . . well because everyone loves their mothers. In the phallic phase, in which a certain kind of narcissistic interest centers on the genitals, this becomes a wish to take the father's place in the scene of loving the mother. This is the initiating moment of the Oedipus complex, and this its "active" or "positive" version; there is also, as Freud reminds us, the "passive" or "negative" side to the boy's Oedipus, "in accordance with [his]"—with everyone's—"bisexual constitution," by which the boy also wants to take his mother's place as his father's love object.

This situation with these two complexive aspects persists for a while. At some point, the boy catches sight of a girl's genitals and registers, dimly, that she doesn't have a penis—or, he sort of registers it, but sort of doesn't. It's not an easy thing to learn, for a boy. "When a little boy first catches sight of a girl's genital region, he begins by showing irresolution and lack of interest; he sees nothing or disavows what he has seen, he softens it down or looks about for expedients for bringing it into line with his expectations." Probably, there really is one there, I'm just not seeing it. Or, it's very small, and will grow later. Yet the idea that the boy, as Freud says, "sees nothing" means not only that he makes a mistake but also that he refuses to see the very lack that is so threatening. But had the boy truly seen nothing, he would have seen clearly.

Later, under some threat of castration (in Freud's day, a nurse or nanny threatening to bite off the boy's penis as a deterrent for masturbation, or whatever) the boy comes to register, retroactively, the possibility of castration that he had managed previously to ignore, as evidenced by the girl's genitals. This changes everything.

> But now his acceptance of the possibility of castration, his recognition that women were castrated, made an end of both possible ways of obtaining satisfaction from the Oedipus complex. For both of them entailed the loss of his penis—the masculine [or "positive," or "active"] one as a resulting punishment and the feminine ["negative," "passive"] one as a precondition.

The emergence of castration marks the internal impossibility of the Oedipus complex for the boy: he recognizes the impossibility of attaining satisfaction from either his father or his mother without the loss of his penis, either as "resulting punishment" or as "precondition." In other words, copulating with your mother would bring the punishment of castration from your father, while copulating with your father would assume castration from the get-go. Castration occurs in the first instance as effect; in the second, as prerequisite. Both are literalist assumptions (maybe the boy's, maybe Freud's) born from castration as an ambassador of limitation, the messenger of the incest taboo. In any event for most boys, the threat of castration from the punishing father emerges as a phantasm that then pushes the boy into a new psychic arrangement. In the conflict between his narcissism and his libido—between his love for his body and his love for his objects— he chooses himself, and "the child's ego turns away from the Oedipus complex."

It's hard to tell how Freud conceives of this final action. Throughout the "Dissolution" paper, he summons a whole panoply of verbs to articulate the boy's rejection of Oedipus: not only does the ego "turn away" but the complex is also "destroyed," "abolished," and even "smashed to pieces" by the threat of castration. Freud is fumbling here, as evidenced not only by the proliferation of verbs but also by the extent to which, in his passive constructions, it is perfectly unclear what agency is doing the so-called destroying. At one point Freud says that the ego's turning away from Oedipus might rightly be named repression, except that "later repressions come about for the most part with the participation of the superego, which in this case is only just being formed." Hm. At the same time, the whole process is also "more than a repression"—that is, if it is "ideally carried out," it is equal to a destruction, an abolition. What to do here? In the boy, in the ideal situation, the action that somehow smashes the Oedipus complex to bits and ushers the child into latency—a repression that is more than a repression, a repression that admits no return—is effected without the help of the agency that this originary destruction creates, and that effects all subsequent repressions. Perhaps, with the boy, things don't get as smashed to bits as they seem? Perhaps there is no ideal boy?

But at least in theory, what we end up with, in the boy, is a situation in which the crisis of castration ushers the end of Oedipus. Perhaps the boy hesitates in registering castration as long as he does in order to enjoy his complex as long as he can. At the end of Oedipus, culture is born. Identifications come to take the place of libidinal cathexes onto the parents, one of which is the germ of the superego; and a broader investment in civilization is effected. This then is "a victory of the race over the individual." Where would civilization be without the penis? Thank goodness for the boy's narcissistic investments! The superego, conscience, culture, the preservation of the human race—all are protests against castration, all are in the game of ensuring the integrity of the penis.

And yet, one must always be careful reading Freud, and not accuse him too quickly. His theories are often a little ironic, as much as they point to the ironies in the phantasms they both hearken to and expose, whatever their broader claims. He switches registers very subtly; he goes in and out of self-knowledge. You never know whose penis he's talking about.

And anyway, even as Freud does describe it, this victory on the grounds of Oedipus is inevitably compromised, since in preserving the penis, you register the impossibility of getting what you really want from either Mom or Dad. "The whole process has, on the one hand, preserved the genital organ . . . and, on the other, has paralyzed it—has removed its function." Much good that does.

*   *   *

Lacan expresses the end result of the Oedipus complex, as it bears on the boy's relationship to his genital organ, in terms of timing, and real estate. If all goes well, the boy

> can become himself . . . a little male who—if I may say—has already got the deeds in his pocket, has a reserve on the business. When the time comes, if things go well, if the little pigs do not eat him up, at the moment of puberty, he has his penis all ready with his certificate: "Daddy is the one who has conferred it on me at the right time."

"It does not happen like that," he adds, "if a neurosis breaks out because precisely there is something irregular in the deeds in question."

The word "normal" permeates the seminars in which Lacan talks about Oedipus, though who knows where he really comes down on it. Though on the one hand neurosis indicates an irregularity in Oedipus, the normalizing and normative effects of Oedipus themselves necessarily contain the irregularities of the neurotic choice. There are indeed, as Lacan says, "quite normal Oedipus complexes, normal in the two senses, normal in so far as they are normalizing on the one hand, and normal also in so far as they denormalize, I mean by their neurotogenic effect."

*   *   *

On the one hand, castration is a fantasy, or a mistake: girls are of course not actually castrated. This is the register on which Freud is dealing with it in his essays. And yet as Lacan says, "Castration is a real operation that is introduced through the incidence of a signifier, no matter which, into the sexual relation." That is, castration indexes the lack that is introduced by language. This would be to understand Oedipus, with Lacan, as the institution of the Symbolic, and as the moment at which language is established and made extimate. Thus, "To speak about the Oedipus complex is to introduce as essential the function of the father." The father is not so much the guy who is there, or not there; who takes you to baseball games, or doesn't; who grills, or does the laundry, or spanks you, or teaches you Latin, or says "I love you." In Oedipus, in the neurotic, the father is the anchoring moment that secures the functioning of language, and of law, and that creates the subject of the unconscious and of desire.

For Lacan, the father in the Oedipus complex further serves as a bulwark against the mother and her desire. There is always the danger, with mothers, that you will get eaten up. "A huge crocodile in whose jaws you are—that's the mother. One never knows what might suddenly come over her and make her shut her trap."

This then would be to the extent that the mother's desire is for the child. A girl does often want a baby but she wants other things too, which registration makes all the difference. If all goes well, the baby does not experience the mother as having closed her trap; if all goes well, she's not quite there, she comes and goes, she is preoccupied, her attention is elsewhere, but where? If all goes well, the child wonders what it is that the mother wants, other than him. The phallus, as it is associated with the father, is the signifier that comes to stand in for this mysterious something else that the mother wants; it is "a roller, made out of stone of course, which is there, potentially, at the level of her trap, and it acts as a restraint, as a wedge. . . . It's the roller that shelters you, if, all of a sudden, she closes it." The phallus is both the signifier of the mother's desire and the protection from it.

And yet it is also the case, as Lacan says elsewhere, that "if the mother's desire *is* for the phallus, the child wants to be the phallus in order to satisfy her desire." The baby identifies with the thing that the mother wants, the thing that might rescue him precisely by not being him, if he lets it. He wants so much to be the very thing that might take her away from him, so that she won't leave, so that there is no lack. Certainly, the phallus can't act as a roller to protect you from your mother's jaws if you are aiming to be it. What Lacan calls the paternal metaphor is then the incursion of a law that allows the child to give up his quest to be the mother's phallus; this is castration. Thus it becomes possible to take up the phallus, for a moment, before allowing it to fall away, or pass to elsewhere.

*   *   *

I tend to find myself agreeing with all sides in debates on Freudian-Lacanian phallocentrism: their participation in as much as their explanation of the reign of its logic, some critics emphasizing the former, some the latter. Perhaps I am just wishy-washy.

*   *   *

With Oedipus for little girls, says Freud, things go differently than they go for boys. The difference inheres in the order of operations. Whereas castration pushes the boy out of Oedipus, it pushes the girl in. At the beginning, little girls love their mothers because . . . well because everyone loves their mothers. Then, she sees a penis. This changes everything. Whereas the boy's vision of the girl's genitals "causes confusion and delay" (to quote the *Thomas the Train* television series that my sons watch), the "little girl behaves differently. She makes her judgment and her decision in a flash. She has seen it and knows that she is without it and wants to have it."

Is this because what she has seen is so obviously superior to her own "unsatisfactory" appurtenance? Or is something else at stake?

The registration of castration intervenes on the girl's dyadic love affair with her mother, which interruption is then contemporaneous with a shift in the girl's investment in the penis she so covets: "Now the girl's libido slips into a new position along the line—there is no other way of putting it—of the equation 'penis-child.'" Freud is almost embarrassed by this formulation, but so it goes. She starts to want a child as an effect of wanting a penis, and turns to her father as love object, to that end; her mother becomes envied rival. "The girl has turned into a little woman."

Perhaps these instances are sequential: seeing the boy's genitals; becoming subject to penis envy; being sundered from the mother; "slipping" to a desire for a baby and love for the father; being born as a woman. Perhaps they happen, essentially, in a flash. It is hard to tell how Freud measures time, especially for the girl, or to what extent such a measurement is apposite.

There are various ways to articulate the differences in these events and their effects, in Oedipus and castration, as they are played out in boys and girls. As Freud says, while "in girls the Oedipus complex is a secondary formation"—a constellation with a history, caused by the emergence of the castration complex—in boys Oedipus is, somehow, primary, outside of a traceable causation: a mythic arrangement, with no discernible beginning. This position then shifts for the boy at the moment of castration, when time—hesitation, procrastination—emerges in a big way; and eventually, this constellation ends. In girls, on the other hand, for whom castration has already intervened, there is no motivation to end Oedipus, or any index for its decline. Thus all of these differences between boys and girls—these asymmetrical positions with respect to beginnings and endings, to what is primary and what is secondary, and to a location in time, which may insist on girls somewhat less precisely because there is no place outside of it—essentially come down to their different positions with respect to castration. They "correspond . . . to the difference between a castration that has been carried out and one that has merely been threatened."

One is easily appalled by Freud's vocabulary, when it comes to the position of the girl in sexual difference. Her "unsatisfactory" genitals; the effect of accomplished castration as opposed to its having been "merely" threatened to the boy, as though he were off the hook; the slippages between the language of fantasy and the language of reality or biology, as though she were truly castrated. The conclusion that, without castration anxiety, "a powerful motive also drops out for the setting up of a superego and for the breaking off of the infantile genital organization" in the girl—the suggestion, that is, that the girl does not develop a conscience, an investment in civilization and culture, or even any kind of genuine sexual maturity. The insistent use of the word "ideal" with respect to boys, despite the admission that not only women but also most men are "far behind the masculine ideal" of sexual maturity and a conscientious devotion to the human race. Individual men may fall short, but the masculine ideal presents itself nonetheless, as such. This notion is elaborated in a paragraph in which Freud insists that for the sake of the psychoanalytic pursuit of unconscious truth, "we must not allow ourselves to be deflected . . . by the denials of the feminists, who are anxious to force us to regard the two sexes as completely equal in position and worth."

Oh dear. One can certainly see what the trouble has been. And yet, one must also, always, retain one's position and ethic as a reader. And, again, one should not be too hasty about Freud, who always undercuts himself, for better or worse. Parse all of these moments. The girl's perception of her "unsatisfactory" genitals—in Freud's text, this is an instance of free indirect discourse. The word is the girl's, not Freud's. Castration for the boy is "merely" threatened; and yet one leaves these essays with the distinct impression that this threat is far from mere. It inhibits, it restricts, it leaves one with an organ one can't use, it leads to procrastinations, demurrals of all sorts. . . . This as opposed to the girl's flash of judgment and insight: she sees and knows and wants, in an instant. Does this flash really serve to prop up the obvious superiority of the thing she so wants? Or, in the essay, does it testify instead to her distinctive ability to work with her desire?

The girl has no reason to leave Oedipus, the girl does not get forced into culture and conscience, the girl becomes a woman for whom "the level of what is ethically normal is different from what it is in men." And yet, what this means is that the superego of the woman—whoever she is, whatever it means to be her—"is never so inexorable, so impersonal, so independent of its emotional origins as we require it to be in men." This then is a superego that won't kill you. Who knows what Freud was thinking as he wrote all this, but his text speaks, and what one hears is that the girl's trajectory is far from unsatisfactory—even or especially in the notion that she "slips." That is, she slips from one object to another, a subject of desire, as Oedipus and castration have made her; and, she slips on the unconscious and in language, and as we know no treatment is possible without slips.

For that matter, if the corollary of the girl's location in the field of want is the boy's in the field of fact—knowledge and mistake, seeing and not seeing, getting something wrong or getting something right—it is hard not to admit that the girl's position sounds more fun. Part of what is notable about the girl is that she does not make generalities. That is, she assumes not that all girls don't have penises, but merely that she doesn't. She assumes there are no other creatures like her. She does not locate herself in the realm of general knowledge; as much as she participates in phallic logic (if she is incomplete, completion must be possible), she also retains her position in the specificity of her desire. Thus to hearken to general knowledge or to questions of truth and error is itself coded masculine; in psychoanalysis as outside of it, femininity and the mystery of sexual difference cannot be known (Freud: women's sex lives are the "'dark continent'" of psychoanalysis), because to know something about an All necessarily puts one on a certain side within sexuation in the first place. There is no way out of this gap. (I learned these things in a class that I took with my analyst and her boyfriend.)

And yet, my question remains: Where then does the woman, whoever she is, in the rigor of her desire, place herself with respect to theory? That is, how can a certain feminine intervention articulate the coordinates of theory as distinguishable from something like general knowledge?

*   *   *

Cixous: "It is impossible to *define* a feminine practice of writing, and this is an impossibility that will remain, for this practice can never be theorized, enclosed, coded—which doesn't mean that it doesn't exist. But it will always surpass the discourses that regulate the phallocentric system: it does and will take place in areas other than those subordinated to philosophico-theoretical domination."

*   *   *

"In little girls," says Freud, "the Oedipus complex raises one problem more than in boys." In both cases the mother is the original object; in boys, we have seen how she is retained. The girl, however, must take the extra step of leaving the mother.

I don't agree with Freud's suggestion at various points that it is particularly hard to get the girl out of Oedipus (because castration does not insist for her, and because her passage from mother to father is yet another move that must be made—itself a heterosexist assumption that Freud only sometimes makes). It seems to me that it's a difficult accomplishment for everyone. When something of Oedipus in childhood isn't worked through, Freud says, it reemerges in adolescence, when, after the tumult of infancy and the relative calm of latency, sexuality erupts once again. It is not lost on me that, in this writing, I am locating Oedipus much later than his first emergence in early childhood: in my adolescent reading habits, in the question of the marriage plot. It is hard to write without revealing more than one is really comfortable with.

*   *   *

Lacan reverses Freud's formulation of who has relatively more trouble with Oedipus. For the woman, he says,

> things are much simpler, she does not have to make this identification [with the father] nor keep these title deeds to virility; she, she knows where it is, she knows where she has to go to get it, it is towards the father, towards the one who has it, and that also shows you how it is that what is called femininity, a true femininity always has also a little dimension of alibi, real women always have something a little bit astray about them.

The idea of "true femininity" here is a joke precisely because of this alibi or wink or bit astray, but it's also totally serious about the knowledge—not factual knowledge but savoir faire—of the woman. I really can see how yucky these formulations sound but I do like them anyway, sometimes.

Lacan also writes, "In truth, what matters to us is to grasp the woman's bond to the infinite possibilities or rather indeterminate possibilities of desire in the field that stretches out around her." And further, "What women see in the homage of men's desire is that this object . . . becomes her belonging. This means nothing more than what I just put forward, that it can't be lost." There is a complex dance here between the phallus and object *a*, and also between being and having, that I don't entirely understand, but I think Lacan is saying, in part, that if we think something belongs to us because we have it, we are getting it precisely backward. What we have—even if we have had it forever, even if our mother had it, even if it's an antique, passed on from generation to generation—can always be taken away. Living in desire hinges on not thinking you have in any permanent way this something to be lost, which opens up the field of the something that already was.

*　*　*

Ivan Turgenev does not tend to be most people's favorite Russian author. He was a churlish type, always getting in fights with other writers, leaving Russia in a huff when his works weren't well-received. He was very interested in form, and in well-made narratives; his works can come off as conservative, and a little uptight. Readers often don't find him terribly sexy, though many think he was brilliant at his craft. Henry James, who called the novels of Tolstoy and Dostoevsky "loose, baggy monsters," loved him. But if his works have trouble letting loose, they are also often about the difficulties of doing so. It's for this reason that I actually like Turgenev quite a bit and think he was probably much less uptight than he seems. He was at least very interested in the possibility of losing his cool.

What do these questions of containment and letting loose have to do with Oedipus? Turgenev wrote *Fathers and Sons*, a novel with the most Oedipal title ever. (In Russian, the title is actually *Fathers and Children*—daughters are included in the Oedipal game, though evidently not mothers, probably because they are at the heart of the matter.) It is a book about family and politics, and about how intergenerational transmission and conflict operate and imbricate in these two realms. Revolution is a psychic act. Russian novels of the mid- to late nineteenth century—when revolution was already brewing—tend to know this; and yet *Fathers and Sons* ends serenely. Whatever the mild turbulence over the course of the narrative (nothing too heady: the son brings a nihilist friend home who shakes things up a bit; the two young men set off for another estate and meet some attractive women), by the end father (Nikolai) and son (Arkady) have made up and are ready to live out their days running their manor together, each with a new wife (Arkady's mother, the absent fulcrum, had died long ago). This then is the marriage plot par excellence: the novel is wrapped up neatly, the disturbing libidinal trends that motored it onward put to rest, or at least pushed underground. The characters who represent other (sexual, political) possibilities beyond a sort of banal intergenerational reconciliation on the grounds of domesticity and marriage are either killed off or driven abroad.

Oedipus killed his father and slept with his mother so that we don't have to. His grim acts instituted their impossibility for the rest of us. Which means, Oedipal repetition is the nicest of malaises: the most conventional, the seemliest, the easiest to witness. What could be the threat when it's all kept in the family?

Yet like psychoanalysis, Turgenev is not nice. It is a mistake to think that *Fathers and Sons* ends well, or that anything is really resolved in its pages. In truth, the narrative is a veritable orgy, a matrix of shifting libidinal pairings, both intergenerational and lateral: Nikolai and Fenichka, a woman who could be his daughter, and a former servant in his home, with whom he has a baby; Nikolai's brother Pavel and Fenichka; Arkady's friend Bazarov and Fenichka; Bazarov and the attractive Odintsova; Arkady and Odintsova; Arkady and Odintsova's sister Katya. Libido is going every which way, and yet nothing gets consummated beyond what either begins or ends in marriage. This fact is more disturbing than it is relieving in the novel, and the institutionalization of eros has a sinister tonality. Something dark is brewing. The pollution is just barely concealed: Nikolai and Arkady, father and son, marry Fenichka and Katya, two coevals, on the same day. How could we be tricked by the niceties, by the beautiful estate, by the sweet spring wedding? This is a dank, incestuous affair.

Turgenev himself never married. He had a child with a serf, and a lifelong, likely unconsummated affair with an opera singer. He would follow her and her husband, with whom he was also close, in their travels, eventually installing himself in their household. He never got over her.

* * *

"First Love" is arguably Turgenev's greatest work. Philip Roth called it the best short story ever written.

The tale begins in writing. Two guests lingering after a dinner party are instructed by their host to tell the story of their first love; after the others say their piece, Vladimir Petrovich begs leave to write his account in privacy and then read it aloud—we are then privy to his narrative, which he shares two weeks later. The substance of what follows reveals the neurotic underpinnings of modern frame narratives whose efforts of containment represent sexual inhibition.

Writing can be a truly controlled affair, especially when it marks a refusal to speak. Why the hesitation, the procrastination, the delay— why the two weeks?

The account that follows, which chronicles the first stirrings of Vladimir's sexuality as they are directed, at age sixteen, at his somewhat older neighbor Zinaida Zasyekina, thus documents the inception of his later authorial proclivities. In the garden of the Zasyekins' manor, Vladimir joins a coterie of grown-ups, each possessing a title or another sort of professional self-definition—"count," "doctor," "captain"—who court Zinaida's favor in contrived enactments laden with sadistic undertones: games with "rules," "regulations," and even a "master of ceremonies," and in which the victor, according to procedure, receives a kiss. Adult sexuality thus expresses itself in its cultural ornamentations and structures of containment, which themselves become repositories of libidinal investment. These tend to be the stakes of Turgenev's various forms of (narrative, behavioral) control. In one game, each participant must confess his dreams, and the most original gets the prize. But aren't all dreams original? Or maybe none of them are? These enactments, by which speech is enforced, regulated, and made into a competitive sport, are clearly the original of which the story's frame—"each of us is obliged to tell the story of his first love"—is a copy. They are a kind of parody of psychoanalysis, with its erotics of revelation. But love and its exposures can be scary and in the face of them many of us do want to retain the upper hand.

Is Vladimir, the bleary-eyed boy who wanders into these proceedings, really an innocent being corrupted? The only child of aristocratic parents who are themselves monsters of restraint, Vladimir is sprung from a hothouse of inhibition. Clearly, his attraction to the goings-on next door has something to do with Mom and Dad. First loves do often flourish close to home. As the other guest in the outer frame of the story says, "I didn't have a first love . . . but started straight off with my second," since "strictly speaking, I fell in love for the first and last time at the age of six"—with his nurse.

But presumably if the nurse was first there was also another prototype, further back, in the place of zero. To start off with one's second love would mean that first love is merely a stereotype plate for future copies, an original by virtue of its descendants. Repetitions have a way of multiplying, such that firsts are seconds and seconds thirds. Love is belated. It comes at the end, like in a letter.

*   *   *

Derrida writes that what is at stake when speaking of the unconscious
is not a text that can be decoded or translated, but rather a writing that
only exists by virtue of its replications. Thus

> The conscious text is not a transcription, because there is no text
> *present elsewhere* as unconscious to be transposed or carried over.
> . . . There is no unconscious truth to rediscover because it would be
> written elsewhere. . . . There is no present text in general. . . . The text
> is not thinkable in an originary or modified form of presence. . . .
> Originary prints. Everything begins with reproduction.

He also says that the present is only the call for a footnote, that a given
text can only be deciphered at the end, as an effect of the postscript.

But who is to say that the postscript will come? Who is to say that it
will stay?

*   *   *

What comes late can be there from the start. The supplement has
been doing its work all along. Addressees proliferate in retrospect, as
one proceeds, as dream-time cuts through: addressed parties more
multiple, parties of addressees more populated, than one knows at
the time. One accuses one's postscripts of being late but must work
to see that they were actually right on time. This is what is called an
intervention.

*   *   *

It all starts to sound like a Freudian case study. Vladimir watches a
tryst between Zinaida and his father, Pyotr, in the garden and "drop[s]
. . . [his] penknife in the grass." Later on, again the Oedipal voyeur, he
witnesses a scene in which his father strikes Zinaida with the riding
crop he had recently been using to tame a horse. If Vladimir's loss of his
penknife represents the castration the child fears in the face of the father,
his taking up of the pen in adulthood is small recompense, especially in
its figuration as a stale replacement for the more immediate pleasures
of speech, and for the impotencies that even its wielding cannot correct:
pen rather than knife, and not even such a great one at that. In narrating
the father's sadistic act, words fail Vladimir as he describes Zinaida's
facial expression. What does Woman want? The primal scene, with all
of its seething confusions—who is doing what to whom, who wants

what from whom, is this pleasure or pain—has robbed the child of speech and left the adult a mediocre writer.

In the competition for Zinaida's affection, Pyotr's closest adversary is not Vladimir but another one of the group of adults next door, who exposes the affair by cozying up to Vladimir's mother. In all of these pairings, Vladimir, bereft of the attention of all of his objects, is the only one left with "no one [to] love . . . me." If the "first love" of the title has an ambiguous referent (who is its proprietor and who its object?), Vladimir is clearly nowhere in the game. The story of his first love is not his own—as though it ever is. And yet, there are ways to negotiate these defeats. One must come out the other end of one's Oedipal dramas—having faced castration, rejection, and loss—in order to be able to truly speak, or write.

*   *   *

I got my first email account when I went to college. Email was new, and getting my own account was a mark of my departure from home. I love writing emails; I write best in correspondence. (Kraus: "Every letter is a love letter.") Writing emails has always provided me with a way out of whatever I felt I was stuck in, at the same time that it probably has also promoted a fantasy of correspondence that is part of what is locking me up.

Since getting that first account, I have set many of my passwords, for email and its social media surrogates, as Woodhouse, as a way of both paying homage to my literary and familial origins—the history of my naming—and of signaling the difficulty of exiting them. But in the end, you can't get out of what you're stuck in by writing an email. Just as I wait, patient in my analysis, for the next signifier in my personal series to emerge, I have been waiting for the moment when I will finally be moved to change my email password: when I will at last give up my stupid conflicts over who is in what house or who has what or whether it's possible to have it all ("Emma" means "universal" or "whole"—uncastrated, ugh) or whether to stay in or get out. How hard it can be to pass a word, to see a signifier traverse the body. Now I see that by the time this book is published, in order very simply to protect my bank account, my password will have to be changed, by hook or by crook. This then is what the writing will have wrought.

(Note from the perspective of the end: I have found my new password. See if you can figure it out.)

And anyway, I am not Emma Woodhouse. I am not not Emma Lieber. "Lieber" in German means "preferred" or "rather." It comes from the word for love.

I first learned the meaning of my name in class. I was in graduate school and teaching my first literature course and had recently started analysis—as though that commencement made that knowledge finally possible, though apparently at that point of self-research I still had to be taught the basics in the classroom. We were on a break from a class in which we had been reading selections from the New Testament, and some of the students were telling me about a nice review they had written about my teaching on a website called "CULPA" which I had never heard of (or actually which I pretended I had never heard of; in fact I had been preeningly obsessing their review for days), leading me to repeat "mea culpa" in response to their attempts at praise. Another group was looking up what their names meant on their iPhones and asked me if I knew the meaning of mine. I said I knew that my last name comes from the word for "love" in German. One of them, whom I liked very much, looked down at his phone and gasped: "Emma means 'universal.' Your name means 'universal love.'"

Mea culpa indeed. Universally loved, universally loving—such grandiose identifications are great ways of avoiding the messiness of eros.

But "lieber" is also much more modest: it is what comes at the beginning of an email, or a letter. I am the Dear that addresses the letter, ushering affection adjectivally, commencing epistolary passions between writerly couples who announce themselves in the space of separation, and delay. I have sometimes wondered whether I can only love belatedly, or in retrospect: P.S., I love you; at that time, I loved you; when I began this sentence, I loved you. Yet in all of these various salutations and biddings adieu with their various temporalities—who is early, who is late, who is waiting for whom—where, in truth, am I? Love is something that is sent: "I love to you" (Irigaray). And yet, one must be able to exist as other parts of speech beyond the adjective, or the adverb, or the preposition: as pronoun, as verb, as noun. As the one who loves, as the object of love.

* * *

A good friend pointed out very recently that "lieber" is the masculine adjectival form. The feminine form is "liebe." So "Lieber" would come at the start of a letter addressed to a man. At the same time, if you reverse my name—Lieber, Emma, as happens sometimes on official forms—the letter appears to be addressed to me, as a man.

* * *

"When I call you my love, is it that I am calling you, yourself, or is it that I am telling my love? and when I tell you my love is it that I am declaring my love to you or indeed that I am telling *you*, yourself, my love, and that you are my love. I want so much to tell you." Derrida writes this in *The Post Card*, in which the nexus of love, language, writing, and transmission is given in the image, on the postcard that founds the book, of Socrates writing, with Plato at his back. "What I prefer, about post cards, is that one does not know what is in front or what is in back, here or there, near or far, the Plato or the Socrates, recto or verso. . . . Here, in my post card apocalypse, there are proper names, S. and p., above the picture, and reversibility unleashes itself, goes mad." "pp, pS, Sp, SS, the predicate speculates in order to send itself the subject"

* * *

"*To love* does not exist in the infinitive (except by a metalinguistic artifice): the subject and the object come to the word even as it is uttered, and *I-love-you* must be understood (and read here) in the Hungarian fashion, for instance, for Hungarian uses a single word. . . . This clump is shattered by the slightest syntactical alteration; it is, so to speak, beyond syntax."

"As proffering, *I-love-you* is on the side of expenditure. Those who seek the proffering of the word (lyric poets, liars, wanderers) are subjects of Expenditure: they spend the word, as if it were impertinent (base) that it be recovered somewhere; they are at the extreme limit of language, where language . . . recognizes that it is without backing or guarantee, working without a net" (Barthes).

* * *

The Dora case is Freud's "First Love." The adolescent Dora finds herself on the edges of adult sexuality, embroiled in its shifting pairings, a prop in a libidinal and social economy that she must work to decipher. She is ambiguously bound to Frau K., her father's lover, both women objects in an exchange among men much like the jewels and other gifts that Dora's father bequeaths onto them, as well as onto Dora's mother, as both a mea culpa and support for the affair. The gifts to the mother are thus equivalent to Dora herself, who is gifted to Herr K. in exchange for his wife. While Vladimir never makes a move within these sordid transactions, the moment Dora is hit on she hits back—the slap to Herr K. in the scene at the lake—and runs away.

What then, asks Dora from her position in this web, are these women to these men? What are these jewels, passed through these men, to these women? What does it mean to be in this crew? Where do I fall? Lacan writes of Dora's "long meditation before the Madonna and . . . her recourse to the role of distant worshipper" as a solution to the mystery of femininity that she investigates through her attachment to Frau K. Easier to contemplate the Madonna, to play the role of beautiful soul, than to accommodate the woman as the object of sexual desire. "This mystery drives Dora toward the solution Christianity has offered for this subjective impasse by making woman the object of a divine desire or a transcendent object of desire, which amounts to the same thing" (Lacan). Universally loved, universally loving. The shifting matrix of possession and exchange, of who has what, who is where, who is away, who is at the spa with whom, who is sending letters, who is sending gifts—all these are a screen for this subjective impasse.

But Dora's solution also keeps the circuit in place. In response to Cixous's profession of love for Dora, Catherine Clément says that "to me, Dora was never a revolutionary figure." In her very protestations, in her crises (look at all these crazy people all around me, look at what they do to me), the hysteric is conservative. She supports the system, with her truth. As Lacan says, Freud proceeds in Dora's treatment by way of a series of dialectical reversals, the first of which is to say to her: What is your responsibility here? Not juridical responsibility, but psychic. These people are nuts, fine—but what of you? What in you is answered by being these things to these people? Freud then fails to ask enough this very question of himself, which is where the treatment falters.

Yet what Lacan doesn't mention is that Dora's contemplation before the Madonna occurs as she wanders around a new city alone, having declined the accompaniment of a male cousin. The memory of this event emerges in association to a dream in which Dora has "left home," as Freud reports, "by her own choice," and her father has subsequently died—leaving Dora alone not only to go where she wants but also to read what she pleases in an encyclopedia (as Freud suggests, to read about sex, the best kind of research). Sure, this is hysterical revenge; sure, the virgin mother elides the problem of sexuality that underlies the force of these aggressions. Nevertheless, we should not lose sight of the significance, for Dora, of this moment alone, of this embarking.

* * *

I suppose it's true that only by repeating, or restaging, or at least reencountering the trauma, that one can find the way out.

Over the course of my analysis, my analyst has had three different offices. I was particularly attached to the second one. It was an odd place, with creaky floors, hidden caverns, strange passageways. There was a back staircase but I didn't know where it led, and a weirdly placed window, and things on the walls whose origins I found perplexing: they seemed, somehow, to precede my analyst's occupation of the space. There was a back room attached to her consulting room that I only noticed shortly before she moved offices, a cabinet with items that I only thought to investigate at the very end of her tenure there. That's how difficult it is for me to research the recesses of space—presumably, because I want to so badly.

Her current office doesn't quite have this imaginative pull for me, which is fine. It has done something more. When she first moved into it (when we first moved), the light in it blinded me.

The office has an overhead light. This is the horror of my life. I spend my days and nights avoiding rooms with overhead lighting. Overhead lighting is the impossible. It marks a space that is by necessity one that I am not in. I flee these rooms like a scared animal, and if I am stuck in one, I am unspeakably miserable. I feel the abyss descend, and there is nowhere to go; all I can do is hope it will end soon. Somehow, overhead lighting makes a room feel depleted, contingent, depressingly transient. It shows the items within it for what they are: trash.

The rooms in my childhood home in Amherst had overhead lighting. Not that we didn't have it in the apartment in New York, or maybe we didn't, I have no idea, but apparently something of the trauma of the move became encoded in my fear of purposeful, non-ambient light. By the time I was a teenager, my bedroom was a haven of desk lamps with meticulously curated bulb-wattages.

And yet, history is only just that, and there is no avoiding trauma, or impossibility, whatever happens to you. There was a period early in our relationship when my future husband and I would fight, and I would feel the lighting in the room change. Of course, it wasn't the lighting that was changing, but my perception of it. We would be in my college dorm room (we got together when we were basically children), obsessively appurtenanced with standing lamps from the campus store, and all of a sudden, it would be as though we were being drenched in overhead lighting. All of the standing lamps in the world can't save you from that.

But it wasn't my analyst's overhead light that was the problem. By the end of the first session in her new office, in response to my despair, she was turning the overhead light off before my sessions. Fine. (I did have a fugitive hope that she started keeping the overhead light off all the time, with her other patients—that I had made a permanent change to her office décor.) But then, a few weeks later, she got a new table lamp, something that looked antique or that had an interesting history or was strangely acquired, and I liked it very much, and wanted to tell her that, and maybe I did, but I could only do so in the context of saying, it is blinding me. It had a naked bulb, and all of a sudden, in that session, I felt its glare attacking my retinas, burrowing into my skull, damaging me. I closed my eyes, and the light was still there, its menace everywhere, in every crevice, outside, inside. I asked if I could drape my shawl over it—I have never felt so insane—and she said the only thing she could say: "You can, but you won't escape the glare." The gaze gazes back, and this is the abyss.

The move, and the shawl session, took place when I was a few months into psychoanalytic training, about a year before I would begin seeing patients. After that day, I began covering my eyes with my hand during every session, to keep out the glare. Not that it's really there any longer when I open my eyes—but somehow, it became impossible to speak unless I am in total darkness. Surely there is something of self-blinding in this. At the very least, it allows you to listen better.

*   *   *

And yet—says the next dialectical reversal—eventually one does have to renounce mythic identifications of all sorts: Oedipus with his self-blinding, Jesus with his love, Madonna the phallic mother, whatever. That's not what an analyst is, whatever our—my—fantasies, equally masochistic and grandiose. Enough of the mea culpas already. What are you trying not to see by shutting out the light; what are you trying not to do? What is your responsibility here that eye shadowing may both speak to and elide? What, indeed, finally, of you as a woman? I have zero investment in valorizing feminine masquerade, but we all have to find our way to a position somehow. Several years after I began, I stopped covering my eyes in my sessions when—for the first time ever—I started wearing eye makeup, eye shadowing figured anew. My hands over my eyes were making it smudge.

*   *   *

Was Isaac Babel even a Russian writer? He was a Jew from Odessa, inside the Pale of Settlement. Wikipedia calls him "a Russian-language journalist, playwright, literary translator, and short-story writer." Perhaps there is something here about a certain Jewish relation to language, to the extent that, if you are of uncertain settlement, you are identified by the language you produce. Babel wrote short, strange, enigmatic, and generally autobiographical short stories ("with lies added, of course," as he writes in a letter to his mother): a cycle of tales about his childhood in Odessa, and another about his experience as a journalist assigned to the First Cavalry Army during the Polish-Soviet War. The latter plays heavily on the irony that a short, bespectacled Jew would be riding alongside Cossacks as they perform army maneuvers.

Babel was never overtly critical of the Soviet regime, but as Stalin demanded more and more conformity from Soviet writers, he demurred, at one point claiming that he was becoming "the master of a new literary genre, the genre of silence." He was denounced for low productivity. In Paris, he had an affair with the wife of the head of the NKVD, who, in retaliation, ordered that he be placed under surveillance. He was arrested; had a twenty-minute trial; and was shot by firing squad. Apparently the last words he spoke at his trial were, "let me finish my work."

For all that I retain of the erotic lives of the Russian writers I have studied, I never remember that Babel had such a dangerous affair. It surprises me. Babel presents himself, in his writing, at times as the inward, eccentric, intellectual Jew, hiding from the dangers of the world outside, paling before a genuine engagement; at times as the transgressive adventurer, riding with the Cossacks, exposing himself to the elements. Or, he is always both at once; perhaps these two images are absolutely interdependent. The brevity of his stories testifies to both proclivities: a tendency to hide and a tendency to rush, to jump right in, to burn oneself out fast. Evidently, however, I think of him more as the law-abiding, self-protective type that I am almost certain he was not. This probably says more about my own identification with him, and my questions about myself. But, writing is always a form of self-exposure, no matter how enigmatic and short. And anyway, I always write long.

*   *   *

Babel's "First Love" is a companion story to one of his most famous texts, "The Story of My Dovecote." The latter is a tale of desire in its first flourishings, and of its relation to creativity, and to writing. The narrator, a stand-in for the child Babel, is desperate to own a dovecote: that is, a shelter for doves. This desire is profound, as children's desires are profound, and as they presage the desiring productions of the adult. "No one in the world has a stronger response to new things than children. They shudder at the smell that new things give off, like dogs at the scent of a rabbit, and experience a madness, which later, when one is an adult, is called inspiration."

It is 1905, and Tsar Nicholas is in the process of issuing a new constitution. The narrator, age nine, is studying for oral exams to get into lycée. Only two Jews would be admitted. He is terrified. He takes his exams in a frenzy; he has a good mind but during the test, a blankness comes over him, and instead of reciting facts from Russian history he ends up shouting poems, practically hallucinating from the passion and the pressure—rambling wildly much like his grandfather Shoyl, who tells strange, fabricated stories about the Polish uprising of 1861—until someone leads him out of the room. He passes anyway, and gets into the school.

The whole family is thrilled with his conquest. Shoyl builds him a dovecote, and he sets off to the market to buy doves to fill it with. Right after he makes the purchase, someone walks to the middle of the square and announces that down the street, a pogrom is in progress. Things get crazy; the boy runs off; he comes across a legless cripple who smashes the doves against his forehead. He returns home, face caked in blood, feathers in his hair, to greet the corpse of Shoyl, killed in the pogrom while soldiers were ransacking the family store. The body has two perches shoved into it: one into the fly of the pants, the other into the mouth.

What is more deadly: desire or self-protection; burning yourself to the quick or entombing yourself behind one pale or another? The narrator's childish longings shunt him into a dangerous world, and yet those desires were bound up in a search for shelter in the first place: shelter for the doves, shelter in the lycée, as though the ivory tower could save you from anti-Semitic fury. The birds and fish are at once images of vulnerability and instruments of violence; both creatures, with their particular symbolisms, converge on martyrdom. The boy's mad ramblings during his history test pay homage to this. How indeed can one feel at home in the history of a nation that hates you? Easier to retreat into literature, which tends to be more forgiving, or fantasy, which provides shelter.

I have wondered whether my and my family's attachment to both literature and to ivory towers—growing up as I did on a campus, then moving to another campus, then another, and another, academic home after academic home—has something to do with Holocaust trauma, as it was inter-generationally transmitted. School can indeed be an escape from everything outside: from the life of the family, from the life of the nation, from the drumbeat of history. It took me a very long time to leave school even though, like Babel's narrator, I had transported the danger to the inside and it was hardly a safe place anyway. I was terrified of going blank. What was I so frightened of? It was as though something awful could intrude at any second though presumably even then I knew that that danger was bound up with desire from many directions: desire which intrudes on the organism; desire as it motivates violence, racism, and bigotry as forms of intense attraction; desire as it burns you out, as it threatens you with your own objectal status, you think you're getting a gift but instead you wind up with a corpse. My mistake, like that of Babel's narrator, was to think that there could possibly be any shelter from these upheavals.

* * *

I studied very hard in school and did very well in order to avoid confronting the moment of going blank, the moment of stupidity which is also in some way the moment of violence and of the object. I only went entirely blank once, in my first year of college, when, on exam in a literature course, I was asked to write an essay on "the role of women in *The Iliad*." My head started swimming and language was absolutely out of my reach.

* * *

Babel's "First Love" starts directly after the events of "Story of My Dovecote." Like Turgenev's story, it is about the woman next door. Evidently the metonymy of desire can only travel so far, at the beginning. Shoyl's murder is the background of the love story—the murder that, as the narrator says, "happened without me." Of course the boy was undergoing his own symbolic pogrom—the crushing of the doves—at the time of Shoyl's killing, but he knows that there is some significance to his exclusion. What are these things that happen to adult bodies; what is this turmoil that I, as a child, can only witness, and play at? Where is my place in history?

The narrator falls in love with Galina Rubtsov, whose husband is an army officer. He watches them in anguish from the window and notes, "The Rubtsovs were happy." They are happy because they are in love, and because they are not Jewish. Such passion is not possible when you are a Jew in danger. They house the narrator's family in the aftermath of the pogrom. Galina's husband is a phallic fellow, a fighter, who stands behind her and kisses her neck as someone else reads aloud an article from the newspaper *Son of the Fatherland*. The narrator's father, by contrast, his own father dead and his store looted, kneels in the dirt before a Cossack officer, who towers above him, indifferent to his pleas. The position of the persecuted family in the Rubtsovs' house is the phantasmatic position of the Jew in Russia and the child in general: impotent, passive, witness to the events that harm him. The only fighting the boy can imagine himself doing is in the Jewish Self-Defense Brigade.

In all of it, the narrator watches his own mother waiting out the storm, lying quietly on a bed, from which she rises somehow "taller and shapelier" than before. The Jewish drama is also a male Oedipal one, and we are left with a question about the place of the Jewish woman, equally rejected and coveted. The only organ of the boy's that "swells" in the story is his throat, which has become overcome by hiccups—the most juvenile of convulsions. Hiccups also make it hard to speak. "By nightfall," says the narrator, "I was no longer the silly little boy I had been all my life, but had turned into a writhing heap." It is in this state that he bids farewell forever to the town in which he had lived the first ten years of his life. They move away.

Hardly a muscular coming-of-age. And yet I must remind myself that these two tales of a boy and his education—figured as a form of training that is meant, but that also fails, to keep you safe from the convulsions of aggression and desire—is only one side of the coin, for Babel. Babel was also the one who rode with the Cossacks, refused to repent, and had an affair with the wife of the secret police. He shows us that Jews also know something about eros, and about diving into danger.

*   *   *

Training: what a horrid word. Training by an institution, the Other which says, go here, now, not on your own time, on ours. Potty training, athletic training, educational training, learning to be a little capitalist, better, faster, more. How on earth could this word be applied to becoming a psychoanalyst?

There is nothing wrong with the Other intruding—it always will, in one way or another, though we have many ways of staving it off. Life *is* an intrusion—as Freud says, the organism aches toward death, we would generally prefer not to, but life intrudes, sexuality intrudes. To Lacan, the drive is always a death drive, get me back to my quiescence. Stories of the Other, demands of the Other, desire of the Other, language, law—all are a kind of traumatic invasion. Yet, becoming a psychoanalyst must be a new way of accounting for this history. It cannot just be one more form of training.

I still find it hard to believe how long it took me to say, I want to be an analyst. Talking around it for years, as though I didn't know what I was saying. Finally, at some point, the words got spoken. I applied to institutes the next day. It felt like a tidal wave, but even then, the problem presented itself. "Training"; "institute"; "application"—to do *this?* As a result of *this?* How can I square what's been going on here, on this couch, with those imperatives?

This problem persists. And yet, I have tried to approach training in a way that maintains, protects, pays homage to what goes on on that couch.

*   *   *

A dream, the night before I am to see my first patient: I am walking down the street, trying to get home, pushing against an invisible force. I come upon a construction site, or perhaps it is a crime scene, and cross underneath the barrier, where, below me, lies a peculiar creature—gray, spongy skin, elongated head, naked, and sexless—on its back, looking up. It tries to speak to me and there is both a leisureliness and an urgency to its enunciation; but it murmurs quietly and I can't hear above the hubbub. At its feet lies another similar creature, smaller, unmoving, face down. I wonder whether the first has given birth to the second, and whether the second is dead.

Is this the analytic space? The place is in ruins, and yet the construction workers—or maybe it is the police—cannot help this thing. What a strange environment in which to do one's work, open to the elements, broken objects all around, a half-formed alien lying supine, asking to be heard. The baby belongs to it and yet also doesn't, and I am out of place in the scene. I get nervous, duck out, continue home, to my family and my previous self. As I wake, I recognize the wish to have the courage to stay longer.

Chapter 4

THE GIFT

A dream: there is no time, only a picture, with a caption. The image is of a cartoon jar of peanut butter, with a face, wearing a construction hat, grinning. The caption, as though a newspaper headline, reads: "Snarlag Knows Everything: The Hard-Hat Prestige of the *New York Times* Fire Department." After I report the dream to my family in the morning, my sons memorize the caption and go around repeating it for the rest of the week. I have my husband, who is a good artist, draw this Snarlag, which he represents with spindly arms and legs, drooping eyelids, and a self-satisfied smile, on a big post-it note, and tape it above my desk.

This one hardly has to be slowed down to see its components, snarl and lag, an emblem of what I sense to be the connection between my rage and my slowness, my tendency to take too long, or rather to think I will take longer than I really will. I assume every production will be a slow, painful labor, or that I'm always the last to arrive: caught in the circuit of mother and child, laboring and late. I suppose I think that only the hard-hat fellows, the bearers of strength and fact, ambassadors of knowledge and prestige can move fast. Or, no, it's the other way around—I know that such types are slower than those who don't require such supports. But then why would I identify myself with that crew? Like Frosty, Snarlag is an ambiguous creature that testifies to my confusion over whether I am what I am so angry that I am not. Like Frosty's cold, the lag is the hinge, the symptom by which I transform that snarling rage into a deficiency that I assume is mine, not theirs.

Slavoj Zizek, on Lacan's *Seminar XX: On Feminine Sexuality, The Limits of Love and Knowledge*: "Love is not an exception to the All of knowledge but rather a 'nothing' that renders incomplete even the complete series or field of knowledge." In hearkening to "the complete series or field," Zizek summons Lacan's formula of sexuation. For Lacan, masculine structure is founded on the fantasy that there is someone who escapes castration—someone who has it all (all the women, all the knowledge, all the stuff: the primal father, which figure Lacan says was Freud's own masculine fantasy-cum-theory). Masculine structure is thus bound up with limitation because it maintains a fantasy of no limit: the field closes, a complete set is created, because there is someone outside of it, structuring the border. You never enjoy as much as you could, if only you were that guy, which you might be someday, when you're bigger, or he's dead, except you never get there. "There is no virility that castration does not consecrate" (Lacan).

Feminine structure does not believe in this exception which proves the rule, and this has something to do with love. In that it knows that there is no one who escapes (castration, the signifier), feminine structure is also borderless; it opens up to a beyond of knowledge, knowledge as something that notionally inscribes the dialectic of limitlessness and limit. In so doing, it reveals knowledge as foundationally lacking, in that it leaves out the nothing that is love. "There is a certain implicit analogy here between the feminine position and the analyst's position" (Geneviève Morel).

I have never understood the feminine side of the graph of sexuation as well as I do the masculine side, which is likely the point. Every time I've been in a course or lecture in which the graph is explained, masculine structure is discussed first. When it's time to go over feminine structure, I am always, somehow, out of the room.

*   *   *

When I was studying to take my comprehensive exams in graduate school, I was terrified that everyone would finally see how little I knew. I am constitutionally allergic to facts. I have trouble remembering who said what or where I read what; I get lost easily; I seek the assurances of phallic certitude and then revolt against them, only to seek them again. Before we were married, I used to ask my husband several times a year to remind me what happened at the Bay of Pigs—I couldn't get the image of a band of swimming swine out of my mind long enough to ascertain what historical event this phrase referred to. Midway through his explanation, I would, invariably, stop listening. This, at least, is changing. Not that I'm listening more. Rather, I am asking less.

Comprehensive exams are fueled by the fantasy of knowledge as a closed set, the suggestion that an entire field can be apprehended at once. We all know this is absurd, and yet our anxiety speaks otherwise. In some academic departments, you create your own reading list by tailoring the set of texts that your examiners can test you on; yet this permission to set a limit on the demand to produce knowledge only speaks to the infinite burden of that imperative. In my department, we were all given the same list of virtually every piece of literature in the Russian canon. It's a relatively small canon, so it's a list that can be compiled without wasting too much paper, and also one that can claim to be comprehensive. Except that lists only exist by virtue of what they exclude; except that it was of course way too much to read over a summer and have something to say about. In any event this standardized list was the dialectical corollary of the tailored one: you have to know all of this, and yet, the articulation of this imperative testifies to its own impossibility. This was a much better side of the dialectic to be on. It had a wink to it, a smirk.

My response was to do what I always did: I studied feverishly, anxiously, with sick pleasure, in my own way, making up my own theories, but always making sure to cite the masters, trying my best to remember who said what, terrified of plagiarizing most likely because I wanted to so badly. Lacan says, it is psychotics, as those who are uninitiated into the symbolic order, who truly believe that there is such a thing as symbolic property, that words are things that can be had. But others fall for the trick too, especially in graduate school. I was periodically sent into flights of knowledge-anxiety, looking up people and events on Wikipedia at a frantic pace, making myself ill, one entry leading to another, nothing ever enough—because of course the list was a lie, because what if the list delineated merely everything that (impossibly) I had to learn, whereas it was expected that *I already knew everything else*? Because who's to say what lurks on the other side of a dialectic? By the end, I had made my own list to document some of these deranged expeditions, the traces of my research of sundry people, places, dates, and events that had little to nothing to do with each other—the reign of Alexander II, the various dates of the French Revolution, what Symbolism is, what Schopenhauer said—and taped it up over my computer: the imperative and its parody on one sheet of paper, watching over my labors.

Snarlag, caricature of the primal father; Snarlag, who smirks at the claim to knowledge that he represents; Snarlag, imperative and parody at once; Snarlag, who is not so much a man who believes in omniscience as a woman who "'knows' that *neither she nor . . .* [the Other] *knows*" (Suzanne Barnard) but still can't decide which side he's on; Snarlag, who is still stuck, who is still slow, but who sees, dimly, the way out—now takes the place of that demented list, taped above my computer. He is one of a number of creatures—Marmalie on my bookshelf, Frosty on my father's desk—overseeing the familial intellectual pursuits, and though I still find Frosty's placement somewhat confusing (Father, can't you see I'm freezing?), Marmalie and Snarlag are very dear to me, since as neologisms they represent both the problem and the way out.

I had no idea why this dialectic—know and don't know, slow and fast—would be represented on a jar of peanut butter, but my husband was prescient. In the dream, Snarlag had no particular brand name, so my husband decided himself which brand Snarlag would be, and wrote on his face, right above his smile, what he certainly already also was: Jiffy.

*   *   *

I have always been very angry at Vladimir Nabokov. I know it doesn't make sense, since he's dead. But that's why I'm angry at him.

Nabokov knew everything. Sure, he was a genius. His was a gift for language that has hardly been matched. He wrote equally brilliantly in Russian and English, and spoke French and German too. His books are some of the most astounding linguistic performances ever created. And, he knew everything about them. Both within his fictional writings and in his essays, letters, and interviews, he expresses a stinging disdain for bad readers, who, to him, were those who read in his works anything that he didn't intend, or failed to comprehend in his works anything that he did. By his lights, he was absolutely in control of the language he produced. He hated the idea that any of it could be picked up and transformed through the action of reading. Often, he constructed his works as puzzles, or chess games (he was a brilliant chess player and also devised chess problems), which he intended to be traced and parsed, their clues tracked. The good reader would be the one who would put all the clues together in the way that he had intended.

He was also a scientist, and specifically, a lepidopterist. Beyond writing and teaching literature (at Wellesley, at Cornell), he served as the curator of lepidoptery at Harvard's Museum of Comparative Zoology. This was after he was exiled, as many aristocrats were, during the Russian Revolution. After a stay in Berlin, he came to the States, where he published books in English that became even more famous than those he had published in Russian. In nearly all of the texts, butterflies make their appearance. In Nabokov, butterflies represent design: the patterns, clues, and signifying traces within the natural world that evidence the artistic gifts of its Maker. It is not a religious ideology per se, but rather a structurally theological one. That is, it is not so much that Nabokov's works testify to a belief in God, but rather that he posited a world with an artist-creator whose intentionality and precision were unmatched in order to fortify the analogy with his own work—to posit himself as the God of his texts.

Thus in Nabokov's metaphysics and aesthetics, we are meant to read the world the way we read books, and vice versa. Investigation of the world's mysteries is also an aesthetic endeavor, and a reader and a scientific researcher are, broadly, the same thing. Bad reading and bad research are deplorable because they are failures to apprehend the gifts and efforts of the Creator. They instead testify to a blindness and a solipsism that are the worst of Nabokovian sins.

Something of translation is always at stake: translation which means, being as accurate as possible to the original. Otherwise something might get lost, or confused. His translation of *Eugene Onegin* is a little exhausting.

Underneath it all, there is an anxiety about death. There is no death of the author for Nabokov—he maintains a firm grip on his texts from beyond the grave—because once you are dead, people can do what they like with your corpse. Better to assert an unwavering control. And yet, Nabokov is and was dead, both in fact and in fantasy, since the obsessional's control is a kind of death-in-life that serves as protection from that inevitable fate. (Lacan says, whereas the hysteric's question is whether she is a man or a woman, the obsessional's question is whether he is alive or dead.) God forbid if this were ever pointed out to him, though.

Needless to say, Nabokov hated psychoanalysis. Psychoanalysis teaches us that we are not the masters of the language we produce—and that our genius is the genius of language precisely at the place where it slips away from our grasp. You can learn all the languages in the world and you will still be subject to the loss that speaking institutes. Even the original is lost in translation. What's more, Freud was also, in his own way, a humanist and a scientist, an aestheticist and a researcher. Nabokov was very competitive.

And yet, every once in a while, furtively, Nabokov's texts speak otherwise. One of his greatest novels, *Pale Fire*—about a psychotic who, believing himself to be the deposed king of Zembla posing as an academic in America, steals a poem from his neighbor, a great professor and poet, and adds to it his own crazy footnotes which essentially tell his fantasied autobiography—features a vision of community founded on radical unhaving, a profound loss of control over one's texts and oneself. The psychotic lives in someone else's house and the poet is killed in an act of mistaken identity, and yet something is born of their neighborliness. In all of it, the poet is no more in possession of his own poem than the mad researcher. There is something here that is very close to the psychoanalytic insight—the basis of Freud's Copernican revolution—that we are not kings of our own castles, and that subjectivity is the effect of a radical loss in being that comes with our induction into speech. And that it's very hard to come to terms with this and we might be forgiven our royal fantasies.

Indeed one would think Nabokov would have been at home with the notion of self-exile, given his history. His gift for language may have been a response to the loss of home; perhaps words became his only property, his astounding mastery of several languages marking the assurance of fitting in or settling down anywhere at the same time that it indexed a genuine homelessness. In the end, all of his books are about people who don't belong, and every word resonates with its own self-insufficiency, the impossibility of getting back to one's home and one's things, as well as with a passionate pleasure that must, somewhere, admit the possibility of overthrowing masters, dethroning kings, and unseating authors. When Nabokov is at his best, his artistic gift testifies to the notion that we are all exiles, bereft of our kingdoms by one revolution or another, thrust out of majesty into language and desire and always on the move.

* * *

What does it look like when speaking achieves a sudden registration—when it, as Lacan says, hits the Real? Well, something turns, or shifts, something that hadn't or couldn't be said finally gets said, and this then affects the contours of what can't be said, and the force it exerts. And yet, who knows when it will happen, or how, or who will be its emissary. Maybe an analytic interpretation—whatever that means, I haven't actually received or given that many interpretations per se, at least if interpretation is conceived as taking place on an explanatory register—will do it, but maybe not. Maybe it will be something you yourself utter from your supine position, staring at the ceiling, not thinking anything especially in particular is happening, and then all of a sudden, it has. I remember once musing without particular emotion or urgency on a certain dynamic that I thought was "confined to my marriage." All of a sudden, I was sitting up, with my back to my analyst, because my sudden hyperventilation, which lasted about twenty minutes, had made me bolt upright.

* * *

It took a surprisingly long time for me to bring my children to meet my analyst. Arguably, I had gone into analysis to figure out how to have a baby. This question meant many things. Nevertheless, by eight years in, there had been two pregnancies, two long labors, two infancies with various complications to sort through, with the result that there were and are now two wise and strange and delightful new humans living in my house.

So why, as she said once, did I keep them so far from her? She revised that quickly afterward—"you talk about them of course"—"but," she said after a pause, "I don't even know what they look like!" An odd moment, since what have looks ever had to do with anything, but there was something to it. My shyness to even show her photographs spoke, paradoxically, to the problematic pull visuality still had over me. I could hardly look at her, her image was so terrifying: I had seen her during this time give a public talk while wearing gold glasses and had found them practically too shiny to look at. I couldn't let her see my children because her sight meant my blindness.

Later, in the wake of the solar eclipse of 2017, which my kids watched with special glasses, I had a dream in which my analyst was the sun: the source of all sight, it sees everything, you can't look or you'll go blind. The sun with its gravitational pull, organizing galaxies, everything rotates around it. Lacan's formulation of the transference as a relation to the analyst as the "subject supposed to know" or "sujet supposé savoir"—that is, his notion that the analyst becomes, in the transference, the person assumed by the analysand to be in possession of knowledge about her suffering—plays on this very spatial structure. Supposé, as Gunn says from his position as patient, is also *sup-posé*, placed on top, placed above, like the sun. In an eclipse, the moon, that little celestial body known essentially for the planet it has attached itself to—known for its transference—goes out in front, and it is dangerous to see.

Fine: concentrate it all in one place, up there, so that, eventually, it can drop, and the orbits loosen. Lacan takes from Plato the idea of the agalma: the shiny, precious thing that we find in the object of love, the gem that marks or accounts for the singularity of the beloved. (This is also a way of talking about object *a*.) The analyst comes, in her place in the transference, quintessentially to contain this devastating jewel.

Strangely, when I thought about my analyst meeting my children, I would imagine running into her, with them, unexpectedly, in front of a candy shop in Brooklyn. A surprise meeting, caught off guard: the most innocent of pornographic scenes. See how erotic life permeates, and mutates? It wasn't a store that we passed by that often, and until it appeared in one of these fantasies, I hadn't even realized I had registered it. It's on a stretch of Court Street, near the court houses, where, for some reason, you wouldn't expect a candy shop to be. Nevertheless, in my envisionings, this is where we would meet, and my kids would bound out of their stroller and shake her hand and be generally charming, and she would extend some kind of literal or metaphorical embrace to them, baptizing them in whatever it was she had to offer—grace?—while I, as was characteristic of my virtual and often real-enough scenarios, would be not entirely present. To return me to that scene would probably mean that she would no longer be necessary within it.

In any case I did eventually bring them to meet her, in her office, and it was a little strange, but also quite wonderful. They didn't react in the ways that I had imagined, and I enjoyed the surprise, and the whole experience felt kind of suspended in time, and I finally registered things in her office I had never seen before, and everything felt profoundly not awful, which is unusual for me. I sometimes think the only places I feel ok are someone's consulting room—living is so much harder than analysis—maybe I could just bring all my loved ones into her office, and we could set up camp there, and live out our days.

Not that indulging the oral object, as it speaks back to law—candy to court houses, just leave me alone with this breast would you—has ever done me much good. Living with your family in your analyst's office must really just mean, inviting them into the scene of your desire. Why couldn't I be the one to bestow such grace? But then the hour was up, and my three-year-old had started throwing things, so we said goodbye, and on the way home, we took a route back from the subway we didn't usually take, and I wasn't sure why until I saw the candy shop, so we went in, and it was delicious.

*   *   *

It isn't quite true that I went into analysis to figure out how to have a baby—or, that's one of the reasons I went in, but I wasn't aware of it, which matters little. What one says in the first session to the question, "what brings you here?" is important: as a fulcrum, an articulation of coordinates. How the enunciation of that hinge as it constitutes the beginning relates to the procession of the treatment will differ for everyone, but I do think that for most people, the answer to that question gives shape to the moment at which something has broken through, a constellation has erupted, and it has become clear that life can no longer go on as before.

We had been married for about four months. I handed in my dissertation prospectus, and I broke. I had never broken before that point. Everything had been more or less in place: my symptoms were arranged; I suffered and I managed; I got a lot of work done. After we got married and I handed in my prospectus, I didn't know what to do with myself. For the first time ever I couldn't do academic work, though it was the moment at which it was most called for. I spent some time writing a very bizarre short story about a woman who was either me or my mother, I couldn't tell. I thought, I'll either have to start going to church or I'll go into analysis. I went to a Unitarian Church service around the corner one Sunday; it was sparsely populated, and at the end, a member of the congregation came up to me and said, solicitously, "You know, we have many Jewish members here." I decided I had to go into analysis.

I suppose it didn't really take long to realize how banal my predicament was. Both of my parents had left graduate school (English literature—mostly Victorian) before writing dissertations. It was an absolutely ordinary—absolutely Oedipal—moment, as it occurred on the grounds of marriage. But that also doesn't do justice to its enormity. I think I was always waiting for the instant at which something would finally catch up with me. I am constituted in some way to allow for a sudden destitution. This is not to valorize that structure: it requires a lot of false supports to be in place for a very long time. But, that's me. Other people have different ways of experiencing the eruption: periodic, cyclical, what-have-you. My husband, for example, has panic attacks.

* * *

A dream: I am with a coterie of women. Actually it's just three of us, and we are about to do something political, and subversive—something in response to the recent presidential election. We are outside of a magnificent, gilded hotel, and we are about to steal something. To steal a car. A hijacking. The leader, who has the plan all worked out, is calmly putting on lipstick. She turns to me and says, "Fem Sem Es." It is as though I see the words spelled out in the dream. I tell her, I don't speak Latin. She finishes her lipstick application and translates: "Femme is the Semblance of Essence."

Yet again, the absurdity of thinking that I can't speak this language, as though perfect access to speech is what guarantees the possibility of a well-gendered existence open to others, but that eludes me. As though the one putting on lipstick, in her fluency, is the real woman; as though words can be had enough to be stolen, like cars. I don't understand why I have been included in this crew—I who have never learned to apply lipstick properly.

After hearing me recount this dream recently, someone pointed out that Latin is a dead language. No one speaks it. And anyway, in the dream, I could read it. Thus the paradoxes abound, in my assumptions and my dream's answers to them. For Lacan, it is the fact of speech that creates the impossibility of perfect access in the first place; what is more, what fluency also produces, in the dream itself, is precisely the denial of an essential femininity. Thus to know how to speak here is to know that gender is a speech act. What the woman has, in the dream, is not any knowledge of what a woman essentially is that assures her a spot in that pantheon. Rather, it is a know-how, a savoir faire, a knowledge of how to act, how to get something done. Specifically, here, it is a knowledge of how to masquerade, and how to steal.

In "Womanliness as Masquerade," Joan Rivière is interested in stealing. The assumption that founds both the paper and the psychic constellation that it describes is that there can be only one. The woman who asserts her intellect—the "type" of woman that is the subject of what many have assumed is an autobiographical essay, a case study of a professional woman who speaks brilliantly in public forums populated mostly by men and then coquettes feverishly afterward in penance for her conquests—imagines that in so doing, she has taken the father's penis for herself. Having castrated him, she is guilty in possession of stolen goods. Rivière describes a dream of this woman who may be she herself, in which she "'disguis[es] . . . herself' as merely a castrated woman" so that a male intruder into her home will take her as an object of love rather than of vengeance: "In that guise the man found no stolen property on her which he need attack her to recover and, further, found her attractive as an object of love." This is what leads Rivière to claim that "to be a woman is to be 'safely disguised as a woman,'" and that "genuine womanliness is masquerade."

Rivière starts out her article by paying homage to Ernst Jones, who, with "his peculiar gift" and his prolific curiosity on all matters psychoanalytic—"every direction in which psycho-analytic research has pointed seems in its turn to have attracted [his] interest"—had recently made an "important contribution" on "the development of the sexual life of women." Jones thus is an object of derision and a "phallic shield" (Butler) in equal measure, and the essay's necessary opening gambit is performative of its content: his contribution must be mouthed in order to begin, production possible only to the extent that it negotiates this simultaneous dance of pilfering, protection, and parody. The peculiar gift is both coveted and belittled (what does he know about women anyway?), and vengeance is presumably feared on both accounts. To coquette, to masquerade as a woman, becomes a project that both testifies to that fear and mocks the small-mindedness of the fury it expects, that he could be so easily provoked. Hard to think of a more effective coming out for the essay ("intellectual rivalry with the man, c'est moi!"), though of course, theory is always autobiographical.

The sine qua non of my early existence: I would match or better my father's SAT score, which had been higher than my mother's. To mention that disparity was a coquettish maneuver on her part. I took the test twice to stake my place in that exchange.

For of course father is not the only one in this game of stealing what can't be had. If I was to best my father, my conquest was surely also aimed at my mother, both as her rival and her helper. Rivière speaks of Melanie Klein's notion of the parents as bonded in their state of possession: "At the primal scene the talisman which both parents possess and which [the child] . . . lacks is the father's penis." Mother is the woman who has it all, babies and feces and daddy's penis inside her body, though somewhere the awe and rage at that devouring capaciousness meets the shock at her deprivation—which is perhaps even harder to bear. What does Mommy want? Quick, return it to her, in order not to meet the horror of that question.

Thus the stolen talisman is also hers, or hers by right, or something she should have, or that I am angry to have to steal from daddy rather than having received from her, etc. etc., and it is *"put . . . at the service of the mother."* The act of returning what is stolen thus becomes, for Rivière, a complex tug-of-war of martyrdom and self-assertion, as the girl "wants to be recognized for her self-sacrifices and for having the penis to give back": recognized, that is, both for the surprising secret having that retains the traces of not-having, and for the relinquishment that speaks of the having that is so charitably ceded. But the circle rotates again, since that recognition, given by daddy, then becomes, in Rivière's telling, a kind of secondary penis that, having been sanctioned, can be comfortably nursed. "Then she has it, and she may have it, and all is well." How to get out of this circuit? Maternity, in and of itself, is merely yet another turn of the screw.

It appears then that the problem of speaking as a woman is tied to the niggardliness of phallic possession—intellectual assertion as a zero sum game, to have a thought means to deprive someone else of one, no one wanting to share. It is as though there are three scenes to the woman's performance: first she is castrated woman; then thief or phallic possessor; then penitent ex-con, returning her booty. The final costume of castration both does and doesn't take seriously the stakes of the show. After all, the assumption that someone has to be castrated in order for someone else to speak evinces the fantasy that it is possible not to be castrated—when to speak is in itself to be alienated, out of control, castrated, messy. The masquerading woman seems, underneath the mask meant to protect both him and herself (the mask which says, in part, "It was so easy to take away what I have returned to you"), to know something of this.

And yet, one must eventually make one's way out of this game. In the end, the phallus can't just be something you steal from one person in order to keep or give to someone else or give back to its owner for the sake of revenge or martyrdom or whatever. In the end, the phallus must be something that can circulate freely: as signifier, as language, as art.

Anyway, perhaps the war of the sexes is just a screen. As Butler writes,

> Femininity becomes a mask that dominates/resolves a masculine identification, for a masculine identification would, within the presumed heterosexual matrix of desire, produce a desire for a female object, the Phallus; hence, the donning of femininity as mask may reveal a refusal of a female homosexuality and, at the same time, the hyperbolic incorporation of that female Other who is refused—an odd form of preserving and protecting that love within the circle of the melancholic and negative narcissism that results from the psychic inculcation of compulsory heterosexuality.

The mask inscribes the melancholia of the object lost through prohibition—like all stable gender identities, stable only to the extent that it testifies to what has been so painfully rejected. Thus to Butler, we must rethink masculinity and femininity "as rooted in unresolved homosexual cathexes." Perhaps aggression—the wish to castrate—is less at stake than cathexis, the profound beckonings of a group of women, lipsticked or not. Perhaps all of this jostling around the question of who gets to speak in what rooms to what audiences at what cost is merely a mask for such refused delights.

In the dream, we actually steal not a car, but a taxi. And who, really, does a taxi belong to? A rented possession, unowned equally by passenger and driver. Can such a thing even be said to be stolen? If so, from whom? From the driver who drives; from the company that leases; from the government that issues license? If only I could give myself over to this lawless fun. The yellow cab matched the magnificent exterior of the gilded hotel (one belonging, I imagine, to the new president of the waking world), as if to underline the contemporary chiasmus of capitalism and sovereignty. But in so doing, it also underlined the fantasy of possession that our hijacking would both play into and defy. What is a gilded exterior but one more lipstick application? Or even better, what is gold, but shit? One of the first objects to fall away from us all.

I had another dream, months before this one, while I was worrying the problem of writing, that centered on what was referred to, in the dream, as my analyst's "booty." She was wearing leggings and I was surprised by her sizable ass. Rival and object, homosexual cathexis and intellectual gamesmanship—the question of who gets to speak, who gets to write. I knew she was writing a book at the time (booty/book). My first word, as a child, had been "book." I must have stared at my parents' imposing shelves, like so many nineteenth-century novelistic characters (what secret knowledge is hidden in daddy's bookcase?), wondering how people make such things, where they get the words for them. Do you buy them at a department store? John Reed to Jane Eyre: "I'll teach you to rummage my bookshelves: for they *are* mine; all the house belongs to me, or will do in a few years." A book about a child who steals books from another child who thinks he owns them. The libidinal power of the word "rummage." But books, like the words they comprise, are always falling away from their owners, received by others, to fall away again—always-already stolen, impossible to be stolen. Pirated booty, which, out in the water, wrenches objects from the state. Where better to read a book than the toilet? Penis-shit-baby-gift-book.

*　*　*

There are two books called *The Gift* that, taken together, speak to this war of the sexes, whatever it screens. One is by Nabokov; the other is by contemporary author Barbara Browning (hi Barbara!).

The Gift is the last novel that Nabokov wrote in Russian, though he wrote it in Berlin. It's also one of his longer works, and one of his more tedious. It's a homage to nineteenth-century Russian literature, with references to, and imitations of, nearly every prominent purveyor of that canon, both in poetry and in prose. At the same time, it is Nabokov's most autobiographical piece of fiction. (*Speak Memory*, a "systematically correlated assemblage of personal recollections ranging geographically from St. Petersburg to St. Nazaire, and covering thirty-seven years, from August 1905 to May 1940, with only a few sallies into later space-time"—so says the author's foreword—is, as a memoir, his most autobiographical work generally.)

Most broadly, *The Gift* is about heritage, literary and literal; paternity; and, the gifts of language, writing, art, and love. It features the father of a dead son and the son of a dead father. It is obsessed with the past. Fyodor, the writer at the center of the novel, whose artistic development the book traces and who is periodically the novel's narrator (as well as the composer of poems and other works embedded in the text), can see ghosts. He wants to write the biography of his father, who was an explorer, lepidopterist, and scientific writer who apparently died—though Fyodor and his mother don't quite believe it—during his travels to Siberia and Central Asia. Instead, he writes a biography of Nikolai Chernyshevsky, the nineteenth-century Russian revolutionary, writer, and philosopher, which largely ridicules his subject's understanding of literature. The text of this biography makes up one chapter of *The Gift*. As Fyodor says, he writes the book as "firing practice." In fact, within all of the homage paid to the greats of Russian literature, much of *The Gift* is parodic. The book is staking its place—as well as that of its author—in that pantheon, and it knows just where it wants to be.

It is also announcing itself not only as a work of Russian literature but also as a text, like its author, with international reach. The influence of Western European writers (Joyce, Flaubert) is clear, and in general, the novel reaches for a vision of boundlessness, as though it or its maker could go anywhere, as though divisions—among nations, between life and art, between poetry and prose, between life and death—did not truly obtain. By the end, the book reveals itself as a work of metafiction: the whole thing has in fact been written by Fyodor himself, all grown up into the artist he was meant to be, writing *The Gift* into which he incorporates some of his own previous works in order to tell the story of his becoming. The boundaries among meta-narrative categories (author and protagonist, author and reader, protagonist and reader, author and narrator) are entirely elided. In actuality, Nabokov wrote *The*

Gift shortly after the Treaty of Versailles had changed the boundaries among nations in Western Europe; as an émigré novel, it necessarily incorporates something of the ways in which Russian exiles of the 1920s and 1930s, Nabokov among them, were restricted in their movements throughout Europe due to their lack of a "valid" nationality. Thus the text speaks back to these historical and metaphysical realities. Nabokov did not like being limited.

The Gift is also a story of the love between Fyodor and Zina, his muse and reader, who believes he will be "a writer as has never been before." She works at a law firm.

*   *   *

For Fyodor, the name of the father is everywhere. As a traveler, an entomologist who discovered new bugs, and a researcher who "left his mark upon almost all branches of natural science," Fyodor's father is a contemporary Adam, walking through the world naming the nameless, often after himself—such that "our name echoes a countless number of times." The novel tracks Fyodor and Zina's peregrinations around Berlin, much as Fyodor himself tracks his father's movements around the natural world, attempting to determine the exact route he was taking (from Semirechie to Omsk? From the Pamirs to Orenburg through the Turgay region?) when he died. Yet all this movement is in the service of this primary endeavor: the putting to language of the brute stuff of reality, thus transfiguring it into life. Fyodor writes fiction, but this vocation is his legacy from his father, who wrote the world in his own name. His creation is an effort to preserve the dead father, who in writing himself into the world disappeared into it. The father exists as a dead letter that permeates the soil on which Fyodor steps and the air he inhales, and which he collects as such: as "long manuscript extracts from books, indecipherable jottings on miscellaneous sheets of paper, penciled remarks straggling over the margins of other writings." Fyodor tries to decipher his father out of the texts of the latter's books and out of his own "half-crossed-out sentences, unfinished words, and improvidently abbreviated, already forgotten names, hiding from full view among my papers," all collected during his research. "Out of all this," he writes, "I must now make a lucid, orderly book." But how to compose your father? How to make him make sense? Even amid all these signs, there "is still so little," "there is nothing."

What rescues Fyodor from his tortured rabbit hole of work and research is the possibility of writing to a woman. He takes Zina as his interlocutor. He writes to her about his first love, a "thin little thing, with chestnut hair combed high, a gay look in her big black eyes, dimples on her pale cheeks, and a tender mouth which she made up out of a flacon of fragrant ruby-red liquid by putting the glass stopper to her lips." He tells Zina that she was "your exact opposite": poorly educated, banal. In other words, she was not a reader. And yet, there is something in this girl that brings him to life, and to writing: "It was . . . then that my versificatory illness began." Zina is the thin little thing's successor as much as that one was the successor of someone else. Walking down the street, Fyodor sees "a young girl with a bottle of milk; she bore some resemblance to Zina—or rather, contained a particle of that fascination, both special and vague, which he found in many girls, but with particular fullness in Zina, so that they all possessed some mysterious kinship with Zina, about which he alone knew, although he was completely incapable of formulating the indicia of this kinship." At stake is not "my type," a phrase that Fyodor finds appallingly banal, but, presumably, object *a*. As a textual excerpt, this is a precursor to *Lolita*, Nabokov's masterpiece; love, death, nostalgia, desire, and repetition were his essential subjects. Likely one can only hate psychoanalysis as much as Nabokov did if one also senses it to be very close to home.

Zina was Fyodor's first reader. She first appears in the novel, before he knows her, as one of the few purchasers of his poems. In their life together, his writings become so much the lingua franca that "his actual life in the past appeared to her as something of a plagiarism." As he plans his biography of Chernyshevsky,

> She was completely unconcerned whether or not the author clung assiduously to historical truth—she took that on trust. . . . A deeper truth, on the other hand, for which he alone was responsible and which he alone could find, was for her so important that the least clumsiness or fogginess in his words seemed to be the germ of a falsehood, which had to be immediately exterminated. Gifted with a most flexible memory, which twined like ivy around what she perceived, Zina by repeating such word-combinations as she particularly liked ennobled them with her own secret convolution, and whenever Fyodor for any reason changed a turn of phrase which she had remembered, the ruins of the portico stood for a long time on the golden horizon, reluctant to disappear. There was an extraordinary grace in her responsiveness which imperceptibly served him as a regulator, if not as a guide.

Well then. Oh—would that I could find my Zina. I have spent my life studying how men write, trying to be the perfect reader. Only now am I finally starting to wonder how they read.

And yet, the image of the perfect reader is only that, an image. So why get stuck on it?

*   *   *

In graduate school, I had three female mentors about whom I cared very much. Two of them (in a kind of Dostoevskian or Nabokovian maneuver) had the same name. The death of one of them—a Nabokov scholar, who died in the middle of writing a book about Nabokov and his intellectual enemies, who were legion—several years after I graduated was, in part, what prompted the falling-away of the symptom for which I had largely sought analysis.

Among other things, this event revealed to me that psychoanalysis and life are not to be kept apart, conceptually or otherwise. Life proceeds, death proceeds—Nabokov liked to trace the procession of death through the events of a lived life—and psychoanalysis proceeds: as one of their elements, as a parallel process, as a stage for the conflicts they produce, but also, in perpetual contact, creating and created by the conditions of all other procedures. My symptom would have never fallen without psychoanalysis, but evidently something else in the living and dying needed to serve as prompt. As Freud says toward the end the Dora case study, "It is possible for a neurosis to be overcome by reality," though "we have no general means of calculating through what person or what event such a cure can be effected."

Freud was one of the enemies in the planned book. Nabokov panned psychoanalysis in many of his writings, and his novel *The Defense*, about a weird chess champion with a history so Freudian it's silly, is an elaborate critique of psychoanalysis that iterates several times over. In other words, is the defense in question, Nabokov's defense against Freud, a Nabokovian chess defense, consciously crafted and intentionally implemented? Or is it a Freudian unconscious defense, unknowingly applied against a stimulus too dangerous or exciting? Nabokov knows the implications of his title, which mocks anyone who would dare believe the latter.

In "Vladimir Nabokov and Sigmund Freud, or A Particular Problem," Leland De la Durantaye writes that the central problem that Freud posed for Nabokov regarded the matter of the detail, since, to Nabokov's mind, "a system of psychic substitutions . . . den[ies] . . . the particular detail its rich, brimming life." The author's minute authorial decisions and self-determination are threatened by psychoanalytic interpretation, which looks for repetitions, substitutions, and screens. Never mind that psychoanalytic practice is meant precisely to return self-determination to the subject in question.

To Nabokov, Freud's problem was that he was not a lover of details, which means that he had not only a bad aesthetic imagination but also a bad scientific one. Durantaye gives as an example of this Freud's case history of Leonardo da Vinci, which hinges on Freud's interpretation of the appearance of a vulture in a childhood fantasy reported by da Vinci in his diary, and which investigates references to the vulture across cultures and time periods. Freud builds a whole theory of da Vinci's psychic makeup on the back of this vulture. But inexplicably, though throughout the case Freud quotes from da Vinci's notebooks in Italian, for the detail of the bird he worked from a German translation of a Russian novel that included mention of da Vinci's diary. The joke here is that the novel had mistranslated the species of bird in da Vinci's fantasy, which, in the original diary, turns out to have been not a vulture, but a kite. There goes the case history.

One can hardly imagine a scenario more ripe for Nabokovian ridicule. The psychoanalyst making proclamations about the sexual preoccupations of a long-dead artist based on a German translation of a Russian biographical novel that mistranslates an Italian word, thereby replacing one species of bird for another. The significant specificities of world, life, and text lost in translation for the sake of a delusional theory devised by a megalomaniac out to make a name for himself. The artistic genius whose legacy is subjected to these vulgarities. Freud here is any one of Nabokov's bad readers.

And yet if the detail is the contested site here, we would do well to ask what its place is in psychoanalysis without glossing over its complexity. Psychoanalysis is an art of specifics: the specificity of a person's history, of her name, of her vocabulary, of her unconscious formations; the slip of the tongue on which an entire case can rest. The problem for Nabokov is that these details are often unknown to the person mouthing them; that they are apprehended with free-floating attention rather than with assiduous research; that if they are missed once, they always come back, somewhere else, in a different guise. And that they testify to the suggestion that accuracy itself is a defense or a trick. Freud was not always his own best self, especially when he played the part of the sleuth, yet in the audacity of his faulty research we should hear the admission that, of course, he was all along writing a kind of fiction that also revealed a kind of truth. Psychic substitution—site of the battle between Nabokov and Freud, between literature and psychoanalysis, and also between artist and critic, and writer and reader—does not mean that the detail gets lost. It means that the thing itself, the true object that we seek, is already lost, and that what we are left with is the force of desire that keeps us moving from one detail to the next.

*   *   *

Freud loved his case study of da Vinci, which he called "the only beautiful thing I have ever written." He evaluated it on the level of aesthetics. It was, as he says, a "psychoanalytic novel."

Generations of post-Freudians have either castigated him for his research mistake about the vulture, or apologized for it, or attempted otherwise to accommodate it. Freud writes about the fantasy in da Vinci's diary as an emblem of the latter's relationship to mothers, fathers, femininity, sexuality, art, and science. There is a lot weighing on this vulture which turns out to be a kite. Yet, strictly speaking, for the sake of the case, the conceptual edifice that is founded on the mistranslation and for which Freud is criticized was never exactly necessary.

Freud quotes the moment at issue from da Vinci's diary: "I recall as one of my very earliest memories that while I was in my cradle a vulture came down to me, and opened my mouth with its tail, and struck me many times with its tail against my lips." From there, Freud embarks on a long disquisition on the figure of the vulture in Egyptian culture, on its association with the mother, and on the Egyptian Mother god Mutt, who has both a vulture's head and a phallus. He makes reference to a passage in Horapollo in which the Egyptian theory that there exist only female vultures is supplemented by a theory of their immaculate impregnation: vultures, as Freud paraphrases Horapollo, "open their vaginas" mid-flight and are inseminated by the wind.

Freud further notes that, in doing research into the holdings of da Vinci's library, he found it plausible that da Vinci would have known of this ancient Egyptian theory, since it was taken up by the Church Fathers, whom da Vinci read, and who reproduced it as natural evidence of the possibility of a virgin birth. This suggestion that da Vinci's fantasy may have been influenced by his knowledge of the ancient Egyptian cult of the vulture then provides answers both to biographical and psychic questions about him. On the one hand, says Freud, it suggests that da Vinci lived alone with his lower-class, biological mother for long enough that his fantasy life would have been dominated by her aspect, as it stood at the center of his sexual research. (It is generally known that da Vinci was transferred to the house of his rich father and stepmother some time before the age of five, but the records do not show exactly when.) On the other hand, it suggests that, as the vulture-child in his fantasy, he identified himself with Jesus, the product of an immaculate birth, with no father necessary at the start.

At the center of all of Freud's theoretical expeditions stand the major contributions of the case, which are, as Lacan says in his commentary on it, (1) the introduction of the importance of the phallic mother as an early figure for the child; (2) the idea of infantile sexual research as it relates to the child's assumption and later renunciation of precisely this figure; and (3) the mechanism of sublimation in the work of the artist, and as it revolves in some way around 1 and 2. The image of the phallic mother in particular is the direction in which all of Freud's research into hieroglyphics and ancient Egyptian theology points; and yet, in the end, his case does not actually need any of it. Ultimately, Freud has no evidence that da Vinci would have known anything about Mutt, but this is no problem for his theory since, as he says, "it is more plausible to trace the correspondence back to a common factor operative in both" da Vinci's fantasy and the invention of the Egyptian god. That common factor would then be the infantile assumption that the mother has a penis.

This then is the juncture at which Freud tends to be found most totalitarian: the moment at which the psychic truth is given precedence before the very evidence that is meant to prove it. All the evidence points in one direction, the direction of a certain psychic mechanism or figure, look at how it adds up, but also, what does it matter whether it adds up as I am claiming, because that psychic truth obtains nonetheless, in one form or another—because what I am writing is of course a psychoanalytic novel? Look, da Vinci read and knew something about Egyptian culture which can be proven by this and this and this but really it doesn't make a difference whether he did or not because he and they were formed by the same complexes. Look, it doesn't even matter that the entire theoretical construction is founded on a mistranslation because really what is at stake is not the species of bird in question but the fact that Leonardo's fantasy is rather palpably an image of nursing merged with fellatio.

Such various accusations are not inaccurate to Freud's narrative tactics. And yet, what they miss is the other side, which is the gift of the mistake. *Leonardo da Vinci and a Memory of His Childhood* is a work that, as Lacan says, boasts "the greatest defects." But these constitute a "fortunate fault." As in a psychoanalytic session, the mistake says something true, which is, here, the truth of the phallic mother as object of research, for Freud as much as da Vinci. Obviously, in writing about da Vinci the artist and scientist and infantile sexual researcher, Freud is writing about himself. Thus he enacts, in his own work, something of da Vinci's project, which he recognizes both as his own and as universal. He performs the extent to which pursuits of knowledge are founded on early infantile investigation as it searches for the phallic mother, all research revealing a wish to return to a moment when the epistemic hole of sexual difference was unknown, and thus when knowledge was paradoxically complete. Freud could have just said, look, da Vinci's fantasy is one of both nursing and fellatio—here we have phallic mother. Instead, he takes us on a crazy journey that replicates da Vinci's very tactics. Research as a pursuit of the mystery of sexual difference pursues the infantile place at which that mystery was, incorrectly, filled in. This I believe is what Freud's research mistake represents.

This is not to say that Freud is always entirely on board with his own project. He fights it too, concerned as he always is with the reception of his ideas about sexuality and everything else. He was not always his own best self around the question of the mistake. In a long footnote toward the beginning of the case study, Freud includes a sketch by da Vinci, replete with internal anatomical detail, of a man and a woman copulating, and he quotes someone named Reitler describing the sketch's various defects: the woman's breasts are problematic, both anatomically (only one excretory duct on the nipples) and artistically (flabby, visually unpleasant); though the male genital is fairly accurate, the vagina is off; the uterus is totally confused. What is more, the act is depicted standing up, which is patently absurd ("if one wants to enjoy oneself it is usual to make oneself as comfortable as possible," says Reitler in Freud's footnote); the man looks angry; and there is something not right about the feet. This in fact, according to Reitler, is "the clumsiest blunder": that "the man's foot should in point of fact have been his right one" and "the woman's foot should have belonged to her left side." But, somehow, "Leonardo has interchanged male and female. The male figure has a left foot and the female one a right foot."

Thus, says Reitler as Freud quotes him in the footnote, it is precisely in portraying the sexual act that da Vinci's "excessive instinct for research" fails him, "obviously only as a result of his even greater sexual repression." Evidently, in Reitler's estimation, da Vinci's scientific and artistic failures here are the effect of the sexual confusions that also condition his homosexuality. This is not a good moment in the case study, though it is a revealing one, revealing more of the researcher than the researched, and Freud, after suffering this long quote, writes a short paragraph that approaches the problem from the wrong direction: "These remarks of Reitler's have been criticized, it is true, on the ground that such serious conclusions should not be drawn from a hasty sketch, and that it is not even certain whether the different parts of the drawing really belong together."

Here, Freud is playing the part of the good researcher; what is more, he has his cake and eats it, suggesting that Reitler's views may be true to the case and critiquing his tactics in one footnote. Why not point out Reitler's own evident biases and predispositions (who says only perky breasts are art? Who says you can only enjoy while comfortable?)? From the other direction, why not point out what, from a psychoanalytic perspective, Reitler gets right: that is, that it is possible to draw serious conclusions from what is done in haste?

What Freud doesn't point out, though he might have, is that Reitler assumes that the two bodies in the sketch *should* fit together comfortably, workably. Men have their feet and women theirs; they are different, but symmetrical. He doesn't point out, though he might have, that this is Reitler's fantasy, not da Vinci's. He doesn't point out, though he might have, that what da Vinci's hasty, defective sketch gets right is precisely the extent to which the different parts of the drawing do not really belong together. The impossibility of the sexual relation: everyone always has the wrong feet. Something of that impossibility and the trauma of sexuality is encapsulated in the image of the phallic mother that is the child of Freud's research mistake, as well.

*   *   *

Lacan writes that there is another confusion of feet in da Vinci's painting *St. Anne with Two Others*, in which, judging from the position of their legs, the women—St. Anne, on whose lap sits Mary, who reaches out for Jesus as he grasps at a lamb—appear to be more like a "double being" than independent figures. It can sometimes be hard to tell who is who, with mothers and daughters. One of the subtitles to Lacan's commentary on the da Vinci case is "Leonardo-in-the-looking-glass": da Vinci wrote in his diary backward, writing through the mirror. To Lacan, the Leonardo case study—in that it elaborates this mirror play as it bears on what Lacan calls "a dual confrontation with woman"—is the beginning of the development of the Imaginary in Freud's corpus. Though Freud suggests that da Vinci's status as the first modern scientist rests on his refusal to recognize any authority over his investigations (God, scientific predecessors, even fathers, to the extent that da Vinci, separated from his father in his early years, had no one around to interfere with his sexual researches of his mother, thus freeing him up for unencumbered scientific observation later), Lacan believes otherwise. For Lacan, da Vinci's position "was essentially a relation of submission to nature. . . . Nature is, for him . . . an other whom one must confront, whose signs one must decipher, whose double one must become, and, if one may say this, whose co-creator." "In short, this other transforms the radical character of otherness of the absolute Other into something that is accessible through a certain imaginary identification."

Such then is the status of the Imaginary for Leonardo, who not only wrote backward in his diary but also addressed himself as "you." Yet, this is also the moment at which "the contrast and the paradox of the personage of Leonardo da Vinci" emerges, which is precisely his remarkable capacity for sublimation. Thus it may be that

> in correlation with every sublimation, that is to say with the process of desubjectivization or naturalization of the Other which would constitute its essential phenomenon, one always sees produced on the imaginary plane, in a form that is more or less pronounced according to the greater or lesser perfection of the sublimation, an inversion of the relation between the ego to the other.

Sublimation is a mirror effect; perhaps the artist who sublimates does so by virtue of an imaginary interchange. You can hear this in Freud's own sublimatory work in the Leonardo case study, which he finds so beautiful, and which produces Leonardo as his double. Aesthetics can be its own kind of trap.

My supervisor says that in Lacan's paper on the da Vinci case, sublimation is also a screen for the death drive, and for castration as an index of death; the Imaginary itself being a kind of screen for the Real, something that covers over the abyss. Sublimatory endeavors, as a method of patching over the trauma of castration, hinge in their own way on the phallic mother, the image of non-castration and phantasmatic wholeness. This figuring of sublimation as an imaginary homage paid to the phallic mother is then played out in *St. Anne with Two Others*, in which Mary, who holds the baby Jesus, restrains him from going over to the lamb—that is, she protects him from sacrifice. She is the one who keeps her phallus. And yet, above Mary, St. Anne also restrains her from restraining him, as if to say: there is castration, there is death. This then would be the symbolic order, standing behind the Imaginary and keeping it in check. Art dances somewhere in between the two. This also means that the Imaginary is a kind of sublimation that screens the Symbolic, a shield from the anxiety provoked by the presence of the Other.

This is all what my supervisor said. I didn't really pick up on any of this in the paper.

Ultimately, in the work of Freud, sublimation remains a mystery. The only way Freud can write about sublimation is to write a psychoanalytic novel, which is only appropriate. Yet it may be the case that sublimation is a lacuna in the Freudian corpus because there is something troubled about its assumptions. For Freud, sublimation is the means by which libido is redirected from a sexual to a nonsexual object in the service of sociality and work—thus bypassing neurotic or other conflicts, and possibly even gaining the happy sublimator fame and accolades. Perhaps Freud was too caught up in that prospect. Lacan has his own varied formulations of what sublimation is, but in any case he does at times seem skeptical of its status. Indeed it can often sound more like a compensatory mechanism or energic outlet or screen for nothingness than a thing of cure. Drawing, singing, acting, writing—these things revolve importantly around death, separation, loss, mourning, and love. Yet, they are not enough. For cure, something else must happen too.

*   *   *

I feel that I am supposed to say something here about the sinthome. I had really intended to do so, after writing about sublimation, and I bought a bunch of books on the sinthome, for research. If Lacan is perhaps skeptical of sublimation, he does, at the end of his career, promote what he calls the sinthome as both a subjective creation and a topological element, as well as an analytic aim. Thus the sinthome in Lacanian thought can be understood in many ways: as a conceptual refiguring of the symptom, a move away from signification—the extent to which the symptom speaks—to an interest in the Real of the drive at the symptom's core, and in the subject's singular ways of enjoying; as a binding of the three registers, such that they don't come undone; as a solution that makes existence possible, a prosthetic suture that is also somehow inherent; as a figure for both psyche and psychoanalysis, or for how psychoanalysis follows the paths of the psychic solutions we have already devised for ourselves. The sinthome as Lacan understands and invents it is something that each of us creates as a way of holding ourselves together and finding a place in the universe, and thus the clinic of the sinthome listens for the action of that binding and to where it has gone awry, and attempts to find new forms of construction that might work better. Lacan developed these ideas in the context of his work on James Joyce: but for his writing, which held him together (says Lacan), Joyce would have been psychotic, since the psychotic in particular has trouble knotting the three registers and so needs an especially sturdy suture. Joyce made his by writing but others might do it with the help of analysis or in other ways. Thus despite the shift away from signification in the theorizing of the sinthome, the question of writing remains central to it, representing as it does a self-writing that testifies, as Joyce's writing did, to the nonsense of language as it imposes on being. Most broadly, the sinthome might be understood as a radically new means of inscribing oneself into the social: an autobiography or publication of oneself in which a new genre is invented by and for every subject who does the making.

But, I didn't read those books, and the above comes from notes on public talks that I've attended over the last couple of years. For some reason I'm loathe to say more.

*   *   *

Clearly, I am angry at Nabokov because I love him very much. He hits close to home.

My love and hate of him rotate around the question of this gift which is his artistic gift, and of how he conceives of it. It is so ample. His pleasure in language and writing is so abundant. And yet, he neither gives of it freely, nor avows what he has taken from others. He thinks it is his. He overvalues his own sublimation, his gifts.

Barbara Browning does not overvalue her sublimation. For her, she says, moderation is everything: moderate indulgences (like drinking), moderate insistences (like exercise), moderate gifts. By the latter, she means her musical gifts, a word that she intends "in both senses of the term," and which she calls "pretty negligible." She is an amateur musician, and her novel, *The Gift*—in which the lines between novel and real life are both made negligible and confounded—is born of her practice of gifting to friends, lovers, acquaintances, and strangers ukulele covers of songs that she records on her computer. Sometimes the covers are requested; sometimes they are not. Sometimes they are sent, via email, as an experiment in "inappropriate intimacy"— the activity that, most broadly, *The Gift* interrogates. She also films herself doing dances, some with just her hands, some with her whole body, sometimes naked. She sends these dances via email as well. Or, she doesn't, exactly; her alterego in the novel—Barbara Andersen, the narrator—does. But, she—Barbara Browning—is her alter ego. She makes these dances available online, accessible with a password; the novel provides this password in its opening pages, under the epigraph, which is taken from a book by a friend of hers, who died.

All of it is very erotic.

It's probably clear that she calls her gifts "negligible" both because her music is that of an amateur, and because her videos and recordings are rather small and unassuming—most of them just a few minutes each. In their modesty, they are easy to send out freely. And yet, they are also hardly modest—they are quite naked. The book is largely about a long-distance collaboration that Barbara carries on with an autistic man named Sami, whom she meets through an online musical forum, and with whom she engages in various forms of inappropriate intimacy for something like a year. They have contact every day, and toward the end of the book, just as Barbara Browning did in real life, Barbara Andersen goes to visit him in Cologne, bearing physical gifts: a thigh cozy made of organic wool for the stump of his amputated leg; some perfume called Realism; some pomegranate seeds. And, just as happened to Barbara Browning, Barbara Andersen is stood up: Sami doesn't show. He has lied about his address and other things as well.

The Barbaras are rattled but respond lovingly. She and Sami have been giving gifts to each other for a year. She has made dances set to the music of his voice in his voicemails; he has composed jazz recordings titled after her novels. What does it matter what was real, and what was fiction? In a previous novel, a character of hers had gone on an international trip and been stood up by her lover. As she writes to Sami in an email at one point, "Often things i imagine end up coming true."

There is nothing negligible about all of this. Browning's writing is spare, and honest. It doesn't take itself too seriously; it doesn't try too hard. It's written like an email. Her art is composed in correspondence, always addressing some other who is real, or imagined, or both. And yet, her work, like the acts of inappropriate intimacy that it documents, does not expect anything in return: any particular way of being read, any guarantee of being received. It is sent off to uncertain reception, just as she sends herself off to uncertain reception, in Cologne. If it is not received—if she is not received—that's ok. She's up for the adventure.

*   *   *

Browning's *The Gift* is also a meditation on gift economies, and it references the sociological work of Marcel Mauss, as well as that of Lewis Hyde, who refigures Mauss's rubric and applies it to creativity. Both of those authors' books are also called *The Gift*. Here are some of the nice ways in which Browning metabolizes these previous texts.

> -But there's something even more interesting than the happy story of gift economies as sustainable and humane social models. It's the moments when Mauss talks about cultural contexts within which people think of gifts as animated objects—things with souls. He says that among the Maori, one's sense of obligation on receiving a gift doesn't come from a sense of debt to the giver, but rather from the fact that the object itself has a spirit. . . . He says that in the Trobriand Islands people speak of gifted bracelets and necklaces as dogs that are "playfully nuzzling one another"—which is why one would reciprocate, to let the dogs sniff at each other, because they want to. . . . In his version of the story, gift giving is neither about the giver's magnanimity, nor about his or her attempt to lord it over somebody. Property itself wants to circulate. My gifts want to sniff at your gifts, like curious dogs.

> -"In the world of the gift," Hyde writes, "you not only can have your cake and eat it too, you can't have your cake *unless* you eat it. Gift exchange and erotic life are connected in this regard. . . . Scarcity and abundance have as much to do with the form of exchange as with how much material wealth is at hand." For Hyde, that's the link between the redistribution of wealth and eros. To him, and to me, the beauty of the gift is that, like sex, it confounds our sense of what it means to give pleasure and to receive it. The more you give, the more you have.

*   *   *

Andersen/Browning wonders whether, if she begins "super-producing both asked-for and unasked-for recordings of my uke covers as gifts, [she] . . . could possibly help jumpstart a creative gift economy that would spill over into the larger world of exchange." The idea is that the more you give, the more you receive, and vice versa. As opposed to feeling in debt upon the receipt of a gift. This may have been one of the problems with Sami; whereas Barbara never feels obligated upon the receipt of a gift, physical or otherwise, Sami doesn't like physical gifts. They make him feel indebted. He knew he couldn't handle her pomegranate seeds, or her body.

"In the best of all possible worlds," Browning writes, "the recipient feels compelled to *do* something with the gift." Who knows what that something will be. Maybe the creative gift you receive will inspire you to make a dance, or sing a song, or make a meal. Maybe you'll make something with the same name as what you have received; maybe not. Maybe you'll just go on a long walk and think. Maybe you'll think nothing in particular has happened and then, many years later, you will create something that bears the traces of that gift, from long ago.

Maybe you'll write a book.

*   *   *

One of Browning's concerns throughout *The Gift* is the question of intellectual property, which she discusses frequently with a friend of hers, a professor of constitutional law. For one thing, her covers are technically a form of copyright infringement. What she creates doesn't claim to be original—she knows they're not hers. But, she also doesn't get any money for them, so she's not really worried about being challenged, and anyway the worst that could happen would be a cease-and-desist order, to which she would readily submit. One of the virtues of giving negligible gifts is that you're not too attached to them, once they're out.

She treats her narratives similarly. She knows she does not have property rights to the people she writes about. This means that after she writes a book, she has any of the friends or loved ones that she has included in it read a draft, to make sure they're ok with their portrayal. Sometimes, she says, they have changes that they want her to make, specific requests for how they're represented, what they look like, what their fictional name is. Often they're fine with what she's done with them. Every once in a while, they're not, and she defers to their wishes.

She writes, "I tell people that I may take things from them and put them in my art, but if they don't want me to, I won't, and I'll always give it back to them, maybe it will even be a little more precious."

*   *   *

At the same time, there is no way to avoid the risk of writing. You never know how someone will take you up. Any writing necessarily balances between privacy and publicity, formed in the matrix of the social link. The contours of our productions come from elsewhere and return there through strange circuits. There's no real way to guard against any given response.

Barbara realizes something like this when, having been stood up by Sami, she's leaving Cologne and sees a sign at the airport that says *Gift*, next to an image of a crossed-out bottle of poison. She is shocked to remember that in German, *Gift* means poison. Transmission is never benign, which Barbara knows well. It is here that she announces that, as narrator of her own book, she is planning on writing the book that we are now reading:

> The title of the novel I wanted to write, the novel about Sami . . . and eros and the economy and collaboration and the experiment that began with the uke covers—that book was, in my mind, called *The Gift*—after Mauss, and Lewis Hyde's reading of Mauss . . . and mine. It was meant to be funny, the title, because it's been regifted so many times. Seriously, type in "The Gift" on the Amazon Books page. You won't believe how many people have used that title. And it had all started as a kind of joke, an experiment to see if I could produce a ridiculous surplus of unoriginal gifts of purely sentimental value. Then Sami and I had spent nearly a year giving each other gifts, excessive ones, beautiful ones, and I'd been thinking about his gift, his Inselbegabung [autism], which is wonderful but also a terrible burden. And it was so devastating to think that my gifts, maybe even the beautiful ones, maybe even this novel, might be also poisonous for him, and maybe his gift was also poisonous for me.

It's only now, in retyping these lines, that I realize that my list above, of all the books with the titles *The Double, First Love,* and *The Gift*—and thus the structure of this book—was inspired by Browning's directive to type "The Gift" into Amazon, and her reference to the creative and shared abundance that this title houses.

*   *   *

The subtitle of Browning's book is "Techniques of the Body," which is a reference to Mauss's essay by the same name, about the materiality of bodily gestures, and about how even mundane bodily activities vary historically and culturally. Her book is about eros, and the techniques by which the body mediates it; but it is also about suffering, and the techniques applied to the body, to attempt to account for it. The two are of course bound up in each other—Barbara for one finds it easiest to be in sync with another person when someone's body is suffering—and the prosthesis is an object that circulates in both fields. The prosthesis is also, somehow, a figure for metonymy in narrative. In any event in Barbara's book intimacies are possible, but they must be mediated. When bodies meet, crazy things happen. Though bodies also do sometimes have to meet.

*   *   *

Barbara writes about reading the text of a seminar given by the psychoanalyst Wilfred Bion, whom, I admit, I have never read. In it, he compares patients to books. She writes,

> He says that analysts shouldn't be blinded by labels, like *manic-depressive* or *schizophrenic*. Rather, they should be asking themselves what kinds of artists they are and whether there's an interesting spark that occurs with a potential analysand that might lead to something productive in the consulting room. . . . Somebody asks what an analyst is supposed to do if he's not really the artistic type, and Bion says that if that's the case, then the person's in the wrong line of work. In fact, he says, if that's the case, he doesn't even really know what *would* be the right line of work, since a person needs to be an artist in his everyday life.

She says of reading this passage, "obviously I loved that."
Obviously I loved that.

*   *   *

Where does psychoanalysis happen? Certainly, it mostly happens in consulting rooms, though the presence of an analyst's office with its various accoutrements—couch, chairs, clock, tissues—in no way guarantees that what goes on in there will be psychoanalysis. Mostly what happens outside of consulting rooms—on the street, in homes, in stores, in cars, in museums, in offices—is not psychoanalysis. But, it can probably happen anywhere.

I woke up at 4 a.m. on a recent Sunday to be a "dream collector" at the annual Dream Over at the Rubin museum in Manhattan. Every year the museum—which displays art primarily from the Himalayas and India—hosts an event in which people sign up to sleep over, and to dream. The evening of the Dream Over, participants troop in with sleeping bags and pillows, attend workshops about dreams, and visit the art. Then, they are each placed under a specific piece of art to set up their bedding; a volunteer comes to read a bedtime story based on or inspired by the work of art to which the given dreamer has been assigned (volunteers write their own stories, often with a remarkable amount of care); the dreamers go to sleep. At 5 a.m., they are awoken by a stranger, with whom they speak, for about twenty minutes, about what they dreamed.

This year I was one of those strangers. I was assigned to four sleeping women. One of them was an artist who had gone to sleep under a pixilated photograph of women wearing saris, with nothing revealed but their eyes. When I woke her up, she said, "Where is my dream?" She though it was missing. But then, she remembered: she had dreamed of a square made up of evenly spaced dots, which were really lights that lit up and darkened. They would darken rhythmically, and in such a way that in the middle of the square, when a line of lights would go out, it was as if a mouth had been created. When that happened, the square would emit a sound, the mantra "om." She said, I dream about art a lot, but never something so abstract, because I don't like abstract art. She said, but this was both abstract and real. The mantra "om"—that's about as close as you can get to the absolute. But, she said, the square, it was also tangible.

Another woman woke up and said she had dreamed of the Eiffel Tower. But no, it was fragments she had dreamed, one of the Eiffel Tower, and another of a mala, I was looking at a mala. No, not a mala, a mala is prayer beads, I wasn't looking at a mala but at a mandala, which is a Hindu or Buddhist ritual symbol that presents the cosmos in a geometric pattern. She had stood before a mandala featuring tiny Buddhas the night before at the museum; she had not been wearing her mala, which she didn't want to bring to the sleepover. In the dream, she stared at a mandala with a dragon's face in the middle. When she looked at the face, it opened its eyes, and its gaze was terrifying. All the while, in the dream, she was stroking her mala, which she often does for comfort. Later she said, actually, the dragon opened its mouth as well. This was an odd dream for me, she said. Usually, in my dreams, I'm seeing through other people's eyes. But in this dream, she said, I was definitely me.

A third woman had had a very short dream—a figure, with face obscured, moving its hands rhythmically, in a gesture of welcome. As well, an utterance, in an effeminate voice, repeated mechanically, as though on a recording loop: "you're safe." I generally feel very safe in the world, she said. Actually the only times I have really not felt safe were when I used to participate in a charity event at a homeless shelter, with a sleepover and breakfast. It was an all-men's shelter and I never knew what was going to happen or who would wake me up. In the museum, this woman had slept under a painting of a wedding and she said, I think the painting reminded me of my first wedding. I had a dream wedding, but the marriage only lasted a couple of years. I arranged everything before I left him, she said. I wanted to be all set up before I left so I found and furnished an amazing apartment in a great doorman building. I told my husband I was leaving him, and an hour later, was gone; I met my current husband that day. She and her second husband are very happy now, she said. They live in an apartment building that has great security, like a fortress.

I spoke with these women as they lay, groggy eyed, still in their sleeping bags or reclining on air mattresses, whispering so as not to wake up others. The floor of the museum was littered with toiletry bags, purses, books that had been read the night before; there were the faint sounds of other pairings having their exchanges. I don't know why it seemed to be all women on the floor to which I was assigned, beyond that this fact says something, to me, about me.

Was this the analytic space? I can't say that it wasn't. Not specifically because I was listening to people's dreams, but because the unconscious was powerfully evoked, and because the event was, broadly, a kind of an intervention. It was involved in the effort of becoming an artist in one's everyday life. All of these dreams rotate around certain coordinates: looking and being seen, speech, the gaze and the mouth which are empty or full (Eiffel, eye full). This may have something to do with the context of sleeping in a museum that features not only visual but also aural art; it may say something about the basic stakes of dreaming generally.

As well, in all of these dreams, there is something of the phallus. There is nothing crude about this claim. Sure, these are women's dreams (or so I seem to think), and the horror at what is missing can be read in that vein. For surely there is no need to insist on one's safety by way of dreams and doormen and fortresses, if one did not feel profoundly unsafe; since surely the sleepover provoked the question, am I safe or unsafe, who will be waking me up, man or woman, and anyway are dreams, dream weddings, safe, am I in a home or a fortress or a museum or a homeless shelter? This question then becomes a mechanical repetition that may, in another turn of the screw, cover over a wish, that is, the wish to not be safe, the wish to be homeless, unsheltered, surrounded by strange men.

Yet, biology is only just that, and we all have something missing, which is all that the phallus means: thus the perpetual tug-of-war between desire and the quest for safety. The question of the relationship between the phallus and the penis—between the abstract and the tangible—is impossible to escape and yet also beside the point. In these dreams, the phallus is evoked by the fact of representation: speech, bedtime stories, art. And, in that collective setting, the dreams and their associations took on the status of art or pure text, which I have here made an attempt to analyze as such, not in order to say anything at all about these women, whom I do not know, but rather to work with these dreams as texts in the way I have always worked with texts, that is, to tell me something about myself: my forms of protection, my desire. This is then, iteratively, the only way of coming to know anything about anyone else.

* * *

As of right now, the following are things that, as far as I know, are true of me, but that I long misunderstood or didn't know. It feels important to list them now.

- I do not care very much about houses or apartments: what they look like, the stuff in them.
- I do not think that work only happens during business hours.
- I know that my body works just fine.
- I like erratic schedules.
- I like surprises.
- I do not enjoy writing works of "scholarship." I am more interested in hybrid genres.
- I enjoy not quite knowing where I am.
- Every once in a while, I have mild visual hallucinations.
- I think that the family can be a hybrid genre.
- I trust myself.
- I am very intense.

* * *

Many contemporary forms of psychoanalysis have stopped talking about the idea of cure.

I have always believed in the possibility of analytic cure, in part because I have always believed in narrative; because I have believed that neurotic illnesses present formations and complexes that must be unwound in something that comes to take on an aesthetic quality; and because narratives end. As Josef Breuer, in collaboration with Freud, writes of Anna O., the patient who coined the term "the talking cure," and who needed to get her memories and fantasies out every night to Breuer or else she would be ill: "in this way . . . the whole illness was brought to a close."

And yet, my faith in narrative has a problematic aspect. In the end, not everyone (maybe hardly anyone) needs to write the book of their analysis. Evidently, I needed to do so precisely because I constructed myself for so long as a character in a book not of my own making. This was my misreading of the unconscious. It was, in a way, Freud's own method, part of his Victorian heritage, to see patients as characters in detective stories that either can or can't be solved. But in the end, a proper Victorian detective can't really do all that much. He can get you locked up, but he can't set you free. This is where Freud needed Lacan as his reader. Sure, I can write my way toward something, but I cannot predict my cure, which will come in relation to, but will not be commensurate with, the end of the book. I hope, when it comes, that it hits like a dart. I hope it stings.

When I used to write academic papers, they would always end in a whirlwind: what I had labored through so slowly and effortfully that I couldn't see the way out would end up, as an effect of a structural shift with the approach of the end, coming to a close with astonishing speed. This structure obtained in part because I had so much trouble, in life, ending anything—hence the profundity of the labor so blinding that the end couldn't be seen until it was already upon me. I have wondered if my analysis would be similarly constructed. I feel myself now spinning within the whirlwind—twisting with the force of the transference as it rotates faster and faster, me inside the spiral, its orbit narrowing as I am propelled to the vanishing point of a reverse birth. My assumption is that, once I am released, a new structure will emerge in life as it already has, with this writing, in narrative.

*   *   *

Some books keep secrets.

I think I keep bringing up *Bleak House* because I have always wondered whether my life would look like it. I worked on it and other

Victorian novels in graduate school in part to figure this out. For years I obsessively and rather tediously compared English novels—about the cult of the bourgeois, nuclear family—to Russian ones—in which family formations are much weirder—to see which side I was on. Even once I had done so, I still couldn't tell.

At the end of *Bleak House*, the happy marriage between Esther and Woodcourt is pretty obviously problematic: an Oedipal repetition, the new home for the married couple constructed as a perfect replication of the old home in which Esther, an orphan, served as housekeeper for Jarndyce, the father figure she almost married. The new house is built for her without her knowledge by Jarndyce and her future husband, and she is deposited into it, in one of the text's most ironic phrases, as a "willing gift": a character in a plot not of her own making. Is the problem that everyone else is conspiring to keep Esther in the home, or that she fails adequately to do the work of getting herself out of it, which would mean, confronting better her history: her mother who left, her father a cipher? The problem with not knowing who your parents are is that anyone can be them. At one point she falls ill and spends months in a fevered delirium, her dreams reconfiguring something of her past. She emerges with scars on her face, no longer beautiful, no longer the image of the mother she hardly knows. This has been her analysis. And yet, the mirror, technology of the image, still oppresses her; and yet, she is still in Bleak House. Something has been left unaccomplished.

These are all obvious problems on which the novel ends, and they are, broadly, the reasons that I have always found houses bleak. I am always worried, in homes, in families, that something has been left unaccomplished, that I am in the presence of some dreary repetition. And yet, my distress in other people's homes can only be an effect of my sense of the replications at work in my own. My parents love Dickens.

Nevertheless, these troublesome repetitions are no secret in the novel: they are clear enough to an astute reader. The real secret is more buried.

Bleak House has a strange structure: some chapters are given by Esther in the first person; some, by an omniscient, third-person narrator whom most readers take to be male. Subjectivity and objectivity are mutually interdependent, but split. This omniscient narrator sees a good deal of the community to which he directs his gaze. But, he never sees Esther. That is, Esther never appears within his chapters, and thus within the objective field of vision as the novel limns it. She almost does: in one of the omniscient narrator's chapters, we follow a detective up a set of stairs leading to her bedroom, but, before we get there, the chapter ends; in the next chapter, we are once again in Esther's voice. This then is the novel's great secret, beyond its Oedipal mysteries and its sexual politics, the law making its way up to the bedroom: that in sexuality and sexuation, there is no meeting, there is always a crack or rift. This means something for knowledge, and for the fantasy of omniscience or objectivity, belied already by its association with sexuation.

As well, it means something for cure, which, for Esther, would presumably involve the ability to take on a body in the visual field, and to tolerate being seen in the world by narrators and anyone else. If Esther is the object that evades the gaze, she does so less as object *a*—to be the object that causes desire is the position of the analyst—than as the hysteric who wants to be seen so badly that she isn't. It can be an important thing, to be able to exhibit oneself. But evidently being seen for Esther remains too much to bear; hence in part her post-illness ugliness.

In graduate school, my mistake was to think that the book's problem was this persistent rift in the narrative structure, as though it could possibly be bridged. Rather, the problem with *Bleak House* is that, within all the family formations and domestic arrangements that it documents, it keeps the fact of this hole at the heart of sexuality and homemaking a secret, in order to deny it. This in part accounts for all of these families' troubles, including Esther's, with Woodcourt, who is a doctor but also, in this book about the Chancery Court system in England, necessarily a man of law, and of the home, the wood house.

* * *

Other books come out with their secrets at the end.

Dan Gunn's book is founded on the premise that he is basically telling the truth, even about his analyst's name. Why not? The name is important, as names always are—the analyst's last name, as it relates to Gunn's, says something about the nature of the analysis. We learn the analyst's first name when Gunn describes a moment on the couch, in which he wonders about the possibility of being reborn via psychoanalysis. We are told at that moment that his analyst's first name, Renato, means reborn.

And yet at the end of the book, we learn that in fact this is not so. Renato is not the real name of Gunn's analyst but a name on a poster that Gunn sees in a shop window when he arrives on sabbatical in Bologna. The sight of this name, which evokes but is not identical to his analyst's real name, is the event that all at once makes possible his book: the rebirth in question inscribing itself belatedly in the writing that, among other things, invents the analyst's pseudonym out of a billboard ad.

Browning performs a similar bait and switch when we learn that her girlfriend Olivia in *The Gift* has been fictional all along, and that she is writing, in part, for another woman altogether, who shows up only briefly at the very end, entirely fictionalized which means in true form, as a rock star—the woman who had broken her heart when they split. This means also that the author of Olivia's poems, which are reproduced throughout *The Gift*, had in fact been Browning herself, including a cento that appropriated a line from poet Matilda Betham about being "unskill'd in speech." The false modesty is Betham's, and Olivia's, and (since, though her musical gifts might be "pretty negligible," Browning knows well that her writerly gifts are not) Barbara's—all of these people fictional, all of them real enough. As Browning writes, Olivia is fictional, but she still feels vulnerable.

Browning had to invent Olivia because the woman she was really writing about had found it too painful to be part of the book. She asked to be included only in a cameo, as a rock star. Barbara writes of watching this rock star play at a festival:

> The howl of her guitar was the sound of my mother's desire for death and her terror of it, it was the exquisite pain of Sami's missing leg and his father . . . it was Olivia's shattered metacarpal bone and the horrible ache of wanting more than she wanted to want. It was my own clutching fear of disappointing any of them. I leaned into Olivia's shoulder, and I cried like a baby, and I loved the sound of that guitar, and I loved the woman who was playing it, and when she was finished, the crowd went wild.

* * *

I have a secret. I was not only named for Emma Woodhouse, the subject of narrative, subjected to the marriage plot, the good and ultimately conventional Anglican girl. I was also named for Emma Goldman and Emma Lazarus, two American Jews and writers, one an anarchist and political activist, one who wrote the poem engraved on the Statue of Liberty, and whose last name speaks to the possibility of rebirth. I have indeed always had some questions about my Jewishness: about the weight of its heritage, and about my grandfather's legacy, and about the fear that his story provoked, and about whether self-transformation—a kind of new self-writing—is possible from within all of it.

I know my parents told me that I was named for these Emmas too but I insisted on forgetting it. That I would persist in maintaining an identification that clearly fit me poorly when other ones, which presented all of the possibilities for which I thought I was searching, were already inscribed, is one of the sadnesses of my story. If I have positioned myself in my life as a character in a book it is of course because I refused to see the possibility of being its writer. My ascension to the other position retains the markings of the former, but it at least opens up the question: What will it look like when I exit the novel, quit the plots as they have been written, and live my life?

Take out one letter from my last name and you have Liber, of Latin derivation—pronounced, I think, the same way. *Liber (n.) book. Liber (adj.) free.*

I have another secret. My husband is no longer my husband. Somewhere, over the course of writing this book at the tail end of my analysis, I finally saw what may have been evident throughout to any reader, to any listener. Every analysis ends according to the terms of its beginning; every cure reconfigures the coordinates of the entry. I entered analysis after we were married in order to find a way, over many, many years, to finally articulate the truth of the something not right that we were keeping secret; I wrote the book, in part, though I didn't know it when I started, to make the decision to say it. Only a few parts had to be rewritten, in light of the ending.

I finished this book of our divorce on Easter Sunday, 2018, the day after you moved out. That year, Easter coincided with April Fool's Day. My birthday—the day, in 2017, as I turned thirty-seven, of the book's conception—is June 14. You can do the math.

Together for about eighteen years—as though we had set out to double our respective childhoods. We met shortly after we each exited our parental homes and proceeded to live out a second childhood with each other. Now, at age eighteen doubled, we are once again leaving home.

Some people say psychoanalysts re-parent their patients—that they act as more forgiving, or thoughtful, or trustworthy, or whatever parent-figures, thus allowing a recapitulation of the patient's development on more propitious grounds. Among other things, your psychoanalyst will eventually let you go, which some parents do not. I don't think that re-parenting is the task of a psychoanalyst, but evidently it can be the task of a husband, or a wife—if, that is, they let you go.

What is amazing is that the moment we decided to call it quits, we got another infestation: this time, moths. They invaded our coat closet and did not respond to moth balls; the infestation grew and grew as we kept the closet closed and tried to ignore what was happening. The image of the home breaks open, and in fly the insects, the infests, carriers of incest. These raging plagues bookended our marriage, this marriage where everything was done on the books, by the book, we were so nice to each other, so considerate, so law-abiding: no infidelities to our pain. We must leave this place, but while we're here, let's put it out in the open, that we began our marriage in Oedipus and are ready to get out. How can you explain to someone that life is structured like a short story? That the home really can be the body? That a bug problem is psychosomatic?

Eventually, we had to open the closet and deal with the moths. You said that our marriage was officially over when, just as we did at its very beginning, we stripped off the clothes we had been wearing to tend to the bugs and, in order to exterminate any larva we had picked up in the process, put them in the dryer. This then was the scene that marked the end: in the basement of the apartment we would each soon leave, exhausted, naked, with nothing left to lose.

I was the one who finally called it: called time, said uncle, made the cut. But, you knew what was coming. We had always been playing the long game, waiting until we were both better at losing. There is no liberty without loss. Over all that time, especially toward the end, when things were briefly looking up, we had been reading your poetry. You are a very talented poet. But, it still never worked, this marriage of readers. We were book hoarders, but we had trouble writing, and when we did, we demanded too much of it, or of each other with respect to it. The reader was never quite up to the task. There wasn't enough of your poetry; you insisted you didn't want to publish; I insisted that you had to. Neither of us was right, and there is no righting, but at least, now, there has been writing. I think each of us was waiting for the other to go first.

When we first started dating—oh God we were so young, barely twenty—I gave you a notebook with a leather cover. You had seen me buy it and wondered aloud who it was for; when I gave it to you, I had written an inscription on the inside that said, "It was for you, of course." I remember, when I wrote it, wondering, as I did about many of the things that I said over the next two decades, whether it was true. I was never very generous to you. But I did, always, want to give you something, or actually nothing, I wanted to be able to give the nothing of the blank page. I did not truly give it then, which is perhaps why you never wrote in that notebook. So, here it is now. See what you do with it.

The Last Thing I Want

The last thing I want is to dance
With you in our kitchen with our
Children not watching with your
Night warmth still palpable hands
In their accustomed places swaying
While sing-saying the words
To our latest that was too late
Your wet hair blessing
My shirt and skin again
Only then can we finish
The dishes sweep up the slivers
Of glass I never stepped on
To mark the destruction of
Our temple, O we forgot thee,
O Jerusalem!

                                        Aaron H. Crowell

EPILOGUE

Today is my thirty-ninth birthday. I am getting ready to go to a party held by a group of New York psychoanalysts to which I belong—the same yearly party at which, two years ago exactly, this book was conceived. In the middle of changing my outfit, I hear the doorbell. (At first, that sentence included a dangling participle, one of my mother's pet peeves, for which I am always on the lookout.) Under the doormat outside, the UPS carrier has left a package that contains the contract for this book. It's an express envelope, though I don't know what the rush was, since the contract was worked out over email weeks ago, and I have two more months to do revisions. My only thought is that Bloomsbury was making sure to get me the contract on my birthday. Penis-shit-baby-gift-book.

Bloomsbury indeed. In order for something to bloom, something else must die. In analysis a few months ago, talking about this book, I remember saying that I always confuse the words "epigraph" and "epitaph." To which my analyst said, "Your epigraph is my epitaph."

How much can the unconscious coordinate? How many coincidences can it provoke? Somehow, writing this book has changed my sense of the interplay between inside and outside. Within the small world in which I find myself, happenings and developments have started to seem written: not so much by me, or by something inside of me, or by someone else or something inside of someone else, but by something at the border of all of these. This new sense has not changed my essential atheism. But, it has given me a name or set of names for what I suspect has always been my form of faith, which is a faith in the unconscious, at the same time that it has expanded and put to question my ideas about what the unconscious is.

A couple of years ago, I decided it was time to start working with men. I had spent a long period of time working almost entirely with women: all of my graduate school professors and mentors were women, as is my analyst. As is probably evident from the structure of this book, I find it easier to speak to and about women, at least at first. I was at a juncture in my psychoanalytic training when I needed to find a supervisor, and I realized that I wanted to be in supervision with a man; I realized as well that the supervisory relationship would be an important one, for reasons that weren't entirely clear to me.

(This isn't to say that my female analyst isn't also a man. Among other things, her first name positions her as the son of someone, while her last name is that of a slew of dictionaries, themselves named for their first editor. How indeed can one name a dictionary without hearkening to that phantasmatic figure, the primal editor, beyond the field of naming, unmarked by the language that engenders us?)

I called an analyst who had the same first name as my older son. I didn't know much about him but had read something he had written online about dreams, books, babies, and grammar, and had the sense that he could provide what I needed. He gave me his address on the phone, and as I wrote it down, I felt the palpable twang that often accompanies my experience of the uncanny. I didn't examine it when it happened, which has tended to be both my virtue and my vice: it allows me to fall into things but also prevents me from seeing what I'm doing. Not that you ever quite could.

On the day of my first session, as I walked toward the address I had been given, I started getting dizzy, and got dizzier and dizzier as I approached the building. I kept checking the piece of paper on which I had written the address down, sure I had it wrong. I walked into the lobby of the building in a daze. My husband was walking out. We looked at each other, stunned. I said, "My new supervisor works in this building."

When I got into his office, the first thing I said to this new supervisor was, "My husband works in this building." I knew this was a strange way to start a supervision. I knew that he, as an analyst, would hear something of that strangeness. As an analyst myself, or on my way to becoming one, I thought: "What does this supervision have to do with my marriage?"

I started this book on my way home from supervision one day. I had had the dream about me and my analyst and our baby and, after supervision, realized I wanted to write it, so I ducked into a weird little deli on Fifth Avenue and typed it up. The only other time I ran into my husband in that building was months later, toward the middle of this writing. It turned out to be the day before we separated.

In the months that followed, I dreamed a lot. Some people remember their dreams all the time; some people hardly at all. I have long droughts in which I don't dream, and which I find painful. The distress that I experience when things dry up is one of my troubles. That's the thing about the unconscious: it opens and closes. One has to live with that rhythm. I must learn to trust the interval better. But when it opens, for me, I dream big.

At some point in that long period of dreaming I had a dream in which I was in a huge apartment. It was much bigger than I expected, and though it didn't quite belong to me, it also wasn't not mine. I was in the back, in the parents' bedroom, which had a hot tub. I remembered with horror that I had put some toast in a pan and left the burner on, and was afraid it would catch fire. I ran to the kitchen, and there was a man there, calmly taking the pan off the stove. I thought, he has very good timing. Later in the dream, my supervisor gave me two tickets to the theater.

When I reported the dream to my older son the next morning, he said, of course the toast was going to burn. You called it toast before you put it in the pan. When I reported the dream to my analyst later that day, along with my son's interpretation, she added that when something is toast, it means it's over. She also pointed out the pair of tickets.

I later met the man in my dream. He indeed has very good timing. He had been at the party at which this book was conceived, which I both knew and didn't know. His initials are P.S., which he knows. I have had to take a lesson from Freud on *nachträglichkeit*, and from Derrida on the supplement. I have had to learn that what comes at the end can be there from the start. As it turned out, he had been a frequent visitor to that uncanny building. He is a writer. He has excellent dreams.

I still haven't ended my analysis. This causes me some worry, though I'm not sure why. I assume that, despite my insistences to the contrary, I have maintained a fantasy that this writing would be my cure, and that, as such, I could know or see or understand it in advance. Wouldn't that be simple. At the same time, I now see the ways in which this book has served as an essential supplement to my analysis, a repository for the signifiers that my analysis put into play. Forms of understanding that were prepared by the analysis—sometimes surprisingly essential ones, about my history, my name, my fantasies—only truly came to be at the moment of writing. This book has been a place of self-composition that my analysis couldn't offer because analysis isn't really about composition, or understanding, or repositories. But, I needed them anyway, if only perhaps to leave them behind.

One of the readers for Bloomsbury pointed out that this book implicitly promises material about the father that never comes. It begins with the mother, and so one would think it would end with the father. It's clear that something of the father is still hard to articulate. Perhaps this is simply part of what will remain, some nodal point in my analysis that can't quite be plumbed. Perhaps it has something to do with the function and foundation of language. Perhaps at some point something will be articulated, or dismantled. Perhaps doing so will mark a sort of end. Perhaps not.

Some schools of analysis don't believe in termination—they say analysis goes on forever, until you or your analyst dies, and maybe even longer than that. I have long believed in termination. I still do, and I take seriously the Lacanian notion that termination happens when—after taking her in intensely—you shit your analyst out. I take seriously the notion that termination is a logical instance that is both unpredictable—accidental, coincidental—and yet also entirely of a piece. I take seriously the idea that analysis is something you do, in your life, to make your life possible; that, if it does its work, it enacts a shift in your relationship to your own resources for living; and that, in order to do that work, it must end. At the same time, I see that my faith in termination and obsession with cure have also been symptomatic, part of my general feeling of urgency around being done, my belief in the possibility of a full stop. I'm still somewhat caught here.

The only thing that this writing has made clear about the end of analysis—what conditions it, how it might happen, how it might reverberate both retroactively and prospectively, what it might mean for my life up until now, and beyond—is that, for me, it will have something to do with speed. This writing has happened very quickly, and it has showed me the suddenness of registration, and also that an intervention can come from anywhere, at any time. It arrives express. I had never quite been able to keep pace with myself. Now I can do so somewhat better.

Stuck on the difficulty of composing the father, I had for weeks not known how to write an epilogue. After the doorbell rang yesterday, I wrote the first paragraph of this epilogue almost immediately. I will have finished it today, or just now, in a moment, before going to cook dinner for my children. I don't know how my analysis will end, but my sense is that it will have the feel and force of this structure. When it happens, I'll let you know.

Love,

Emma

WRITINGS, IN ORDER OF APPEARANCE

Jacques Derrida, "Freud and the Scene of Writing"
Roland Barthes, *A Lover's Discourse*
Bruce Fink, *Lacan on Love: An Exploration of Lacan's Seminar VIII, Transference*
Paul Preciado, *Testo Junkie*
Shoshana Felman, *What Does a Woman Want?: Reading and Sexual Difference*
Emma Lieber, *God's Children*
Fyodor Dostoevsky, *The Brothers Karamazov*
Haruki Murakami, *The Wind-Up Bird Chronicle*
Marilynne Robinson, *Housekeeping*
Shoshana Felman, *Testimony: Crises of Witnessing in Literature, Psychoanalysis, and History*
Dan Gunn, *Wool-Gathering, or How I Ended Analysis*
Donald Antrim, "I Bought a Bed"
Charles Dickens, *Bleak House*
Eve Sedgwick, *A Dialogue on Love*
Alison Bechdel, *Are You My Mother?*
Alison Bechdel, *Fun Home*
Roland Barthes, "The Pleasure of the Text"
Nancy K. Miller, *Getting Personal: Feminist Occasions and Other Autobiographical Acts*
Sigmund Freud, "On Narcissism"
Sigmund Freud, *The Interpretation of Dreams*
Sigmund Freud, Letter to Wilhelm Fliess, October 15, 1897
Sigmund Freud, Letter to Wilhelm Fliess, November 14, 1897
Virginia Woolf, "A Room of One's Own"
Maggie Nelson, *The Argonauts*
Judith Butler, *Gender Trouble*
Andrew Parker, *The Theorist's Mother*
Sigmund Freud, "Concerning a Particular Type of Object Choice in Men"
Jacques Derrida and Elisabeth Roudinesco, *For What Tomorrow*
Julia Kristeva, *Black Sun: Depression and Melancholia*
Simone de Beauvoir, *The Second Sex*

Jacqueline Rose, "Of Knowledge and Mothers: On the Work of
    Christopher Bollas"
J. B. Pontalis, "Notable Encounters"
J. B. Pontalis, *Windows = Fenêtres*
Sigmund Freud, Letter to Carl Jung, September 19, 1907
Jacques Lacan, *The Seminar of Jacques Lacan Book I: Freud's Papers
    on Technique*
Sigmund Freud, "Observations on Transference Love"
Jacques Lacan, *The Seminar of Jacques Lacan Book XI: The Four
    Fundamental Concepts of Psychoanalysis*
Jacques Lacan, "The Signification of the Phallus"
Simone de Beauvoir, *Memoir of a Dutiful Daughter*
Eve Sedgwick, "A Poem Is Being Written"
Chris Kraus, *I Love Dick*
Virginia Woolf, *To The Lighthouse*
Adam Phillips, *On Kissing, Tickling, and Being Bored*
Roland Barthes, *Roland Barthes by Roland Barthes*
Phillys Greenacre, "The Role of Transference: Practical Considerations
    in Relation to Psychoanalytic Therapy"
Jacques Lacan, "The Mirror Stage as Formative of the *I* Function as
    Revealed in Psychoanalytic Experience"
Mladen Dolar, "'I Shall Be with You on Your Wedding Night': Lacan
    and the Uncanny"
Roland Barthes, *Camera Lucida*
Fyodor Dostoevsky, *The Double*
Sigmund Freud, "The Uncanny"
Ferdinand de Saussure, *Course in General Linguistics*
Sigmund Freud, "Negation"
Jacques Lacan, *The Seminar of Jacques Lacan, Book X: Anxiety*
Fyodor Dostoevsky, *Crime and Punishment*
Mikhail Bakhtin, *Problems of Dostoevsky's Poetics*
Jacques Lacan, *The Seminar of Jacques Lacan, Book II: The Ego in
    Freud's Theory and in the Technique of Psychoanalysis*
Sigmund Freud, Draft N with letter to Fleiss, May 31, 1897
Hélène Cixous, "Fiction and its Phantoms: A Reading of Freud's
    Das Unheimliche"
E. T. A. Hoffmann, "The Sandman"
D. W. Winnicott, "Transitional Objects and Transitional Phenomena"
Jane Austen, *Emma*
Randal Jarrell, Introduction to *The Man Who Loved Children* by
    Christina Stead

Writings, in Order of Appearance   143

Jane Austen, *Pride and Prejudice*
Samuel Richardson, *Clarissa, or, the History of a Young Lady*
Francis Grose, *A Classical Dictionary of the Vulgar Tongue*
Sigmund Freud, "Some Psychical Consequences of the Anatomical Distinction Between the Sexes"
Sigmund Freud, "The Dissolution of the Oedipus Complex"
Jacques Lacan, *The Seminar of Jacques Lacan Book V: Formations of the Unconscious*
Jacques Lacan, *The Seminar of Jacques Lacan Book XVII: The Other Side of Psychoanalysis*
Jacques Lacan, "The Signification of the Phallus"
Sigmund Freud, "The Question of Lay Analysis"
Hélène Cixous, "The Laugh of the Medusa"
Ivan Turgenev, *Fathers and Sons*
Ivan Turgenev, "First Love"
Luce Irigaray, *I Love to You: Sketch for a Felicity Within History*
Jacques Derrida, *The Post Card*
Sigmund Freud, *Fragments of an Analysis of a Case of Hysteria*
Jacques Lacan, "Intervention on the Transference"
Hélène Cixous and Catherine Clément, "The Untenable"
Isaac Babel, letter to his family, October 14, 1931
Isaac Babel, Address to the Union of Soviet Writers, 1934
Isaac Babel, "The Story of My Dovecote"
Isaac Babel, "First Love"
Slavoj Zizek, "The Real of Sexual Difference"
Jacques Lacan, "Guiding Remarks for a Convention on Female Sexuality"
Geneviève Morel, "Feminine Conditions of Jouissance"
Suzanne Barnard, "Tongues of Angels: Feminine Structure and Other Jouissance"
Vladimir Nabokov, *Pale Fire*
Joan Rivière, "Womanliness as Masquerade"
Charlotte Brontë, *Jane Eyre*
Vladimir Nabokov, *The Gift*
Vladimir Nabokov, *Speak Memory*
Vladimir Nabokov, *The Defense*
Leland De la Durantaye, "Vladimir Nabokov and Sigmund Freud, or A Particular Problem"
Sigmund Freud, *Leonardo da Vinci and a Memory of His Childhood*
Jacques Lacan, *The Seminar of Jacques Lacan Book IV: The Object Relation*

Barbara Browning, *The Gift*
Marcel Mauss, *The Gift*
Lewis Hyde, *The Gift*
Marcel Mauss, "Techniques of the Body"
Wilfred Bion, "A Seminar in Paris. 1978"
Josef Breuer and Sigmund Freud, *Studies on Hysteria*
Matilda Betham, "Vignette IX"

CPSIA information can be obtained
at www.ICGtesting.com
Printed in the USA
LVHW081613231221
707036LV00018BA/202